John —
I thoroughly enjoyed
your class reunion.
    I hope this volume will evoke a
few smiles and chuckles.
    May the better angels of your nature
always be with you.
                    — Mitch Tullai

Football's Best
Quips, Quotes and Quellers

Football's Best
Quips, Quotes and Quellers

Martin D. (Mitch) Tullai

Pearce Publishers, Inc.
Timonium, Maryland, USA
1-800-662-2354
2003

Football's Best Quips, Quotes and Quellers
by Martin D. (Mitch) Tullai

Illustrations by Joseph Sheppard

PEARCE PUBLISHERS, INC.
Timonium, Maryland USA
1-800-662-2354
2003
Printed in the United States of America

ISBN 1-883122-24-4

Publisher's Cataloging-in-Publication
(Provided by Quality Books, Inc.)

Tullai, Martin D.
   Football's best quips, quotes and quellers / Martin
D. (Mitch) Tullai.
   p. cm.
   Includes index.
   ISBN 1-883122-24-4

   1. Football--Quotations, maxims, etc.   I. Title.

GV959.T85 2003   796.332
                           QBI03-200363

Dedication

This lighthearted and humorous look at the exciting sport of football is dedicated with much respect, deep gratitude and sincere appreciation to the many committed and hard working players, coaches and support people I have had the good fortune to be involved with in my role as player and coach. Thank you and may the better angels of your nature always be with you.

Table of Contents

Preface

Football is a great game to play and an exciting event to take in as a spectator. It is a tough, rugged, stimulating sport which holds the interest of fans throughout the nation.

While hard work, dedication and personal sacrifice are essential ingredients for a successful program, so, too, can an attitude—an esprit de corps—which engenders respect for each other and promotes a positive and optimistic outlook help achieve this goal.

And, surely, when a sense of humor is added to the mix, it bodes well for success. A broad smile and a ringing chuckle now and again can be the best remedy for the woes of the world.

Former University of Michigan football player and President of the United States, Gerald R. Ford, has reminded us: "The national costume does not have to be a stuffed shirt. Humor can be the lubricant that eases our journey through life."

And Bud Grant, the highly respected and successful former coach of the Minnesota Vikings, has observed: "Somebody without humor is the most boring person in the world. If you can't appeal to somebody's humor once in awhile, life gets to be an awful bore."

Since times and circumstances change, it should be noted that coaches, administrators, players, sportswriters and others often change their jobs and affiliations. The folks quoted herein are identified with the team, newspaper or position they were associated with when the remarks were made, unless otherwise indicated.

Acknowledgements

It was my good fortune as a football player at Newport Township High School in Wanamie, Pennsylvania, and at Western Maryland College to have been associated with wonderful people.

Later, in my coaching career, briefly at Middletown Township High School (N. J.) and for over 40 years at St. Paul's School in Brooklandville, Maryland, I was privileged to coach the finest group of football players imaginable, as well as work with an assemblage of terrific, hard working and dedicated coaches. The attitude, wisdom, industry and initiative of these men contributed more than I can say to the success of our football program.

These players and coaches made coaching football—

NOT a burden, but a joy;

NOT a task, but a labor of love;

NOT a worry, but a responsibility;

from which great satisfaction was derived.

I am pleased that in addition to highlighting some of the best football quips, quotes and quellers, this volume affords me an opportunity to thank all who helped make football such an exciting and satisfying experience.

Special thanks to Charlie Havens, Dick Harlow, Tom Tereshinski, Bruce Ferguson, Joe Giannelli, Jim Boyer, Lowell Skinner Ensor, President of Western Maryland College, 1947–1972, Walter Serowicz, Arnie Truax, Gene Corrigan, Jack Molesworth, George Mitchell, Mark Reuss, Tom Longstreth, Neale Smith, Brian Abbott, Mark Curtis,

Larry Story, Steve Hornish, Skip Darrell, Clifford Low, Larry Smith, trainer Brett Porter, statistician-general aide Robert Schlenger, Jr., team physician Dr. William Pillsbury, great supporter of all St. Paul's teams, Louis D. Clark, Directors of Maintenance Gerry Spindler, Bob Springer, Charlie Teague and Charlie Ackerman, along with their very able, knowledgeable and helpful crews of hard-working people, and especially four Associate Head Coaches of special distinction: Mike Rentko, Chuck O'Connell and Rick Collins. The able assistance of secretaries Dorothy Hasson, Lois Douglas and Betty Jean Tyler was always very helpful.

I am most appreciative of the encouragement, support and friendship of the four Headmasters under whom I served at St. Paul's. It was a pleasure to work in various positions under S. Atherton Middleton, Jack Ordeman, Robert Hallett, and Tom Reid—four outstanding educators and admirable gentlemen.

Thanks to J.B. Tullai, Linda Bernstorf and Robin G. Webster for their typing and assisting in the general set-up of the manuscript.

A doff of the old Western Maryland College leather football helmet to classmate, teammate and fine friend, LeRoy Merritt, for his thoughtful, generous and able assistance in helping to bring this endeavor to completion.

My grateful thanks to my wonderful family for their constant support and understanding. My wife Jean and my daughters Jaye Ann, Kim Marie, Lisa Jean and Brenda Martin, along with my grandchildren, Lindsay, Tyler, Daniel and Riley have my heartfelt love.

Section I:
The Players

Chapter 1

Sonny Jurgenson, former heralded Redskins QB, invited to Baltimore to participate in the opening of John Unitas's restaurant, "The Golden Arm," was greeted by Unitas, interviewed by reporters and then turned to the Colt great and quipped: "Hey John, thanks for naming your restaurant after me."

Troy Aikman, former Dallas QB and now a Fox TV analyst, about a large lineman's weight: " Boy—339! That should be a time of day, not a person's weight."

Mitch Whiteley, old time Mc Donogh School (Balt., Md.) tailback, relating a favorite gridiron story: "A player calls his coach's house. The coach's wife answers.
Player: "Is the coach there?"
Wife: "No, but give me your number and I'll have him call you back."
Player: "Number 32."

George Rogers, New Orleans Saints running back, asked if he had any goals this season: "I want to gain 1,500 or 2,000 yards, whichever comes first."

Cleveland Browns nose tackle Bob Golic, on why anybody would want to play the position: "You have to be either unemployed or crazy."

Doug Flutie, Boston College quarterback on Terry Hoage attaining a 3.85 grade point in genetics: "As every student athlete knows, that's the study of genes: Jordache, Sasson, Calvins."

Paul Warfield, outstanding All-Pro receiver: "I polished my pass-receiving skills catching four passes a year for Woody Hayes."

❦

John Campana, guard for the Bucknell football team, when asked about superstitions: "I don't like to jump from tall buildings before big games."

❦

Dave Casper, on the rigors of preseason training: "You've just got to force yourself to put your mind on automatic pilot. You make yourself numb as you can. The more numb you are, the better you can deal with it."

❦

John Riggins, Washington Redskins running back: "Preseason games are like military maneuvers using plastic bullets."

❦

Mark Cooper, Denver Bronco rookie tackle, commenting on the hate mail that teammate John Elway has received from residents of Baltimore unhappy over his spurning of the Colts: "You wouldn't think people would have much time for that. I don't even have time to write people I like."

❦

Johnny Unitas upon hearing that Dan Pastorini threw a football from the parking lot of his hotel into a sixth-floor balcony: "You can bet that his receivers were on the second floor."

❦

Cincinnati Bengals QB Boomer Esiason on NFL locker-room access to female reporters: "I've had more trouble with drunks in the locker room."

❦

Larry Cole, Dallas Cowboys lineman, on the plane waiting to take off, following the game with San Diego, in which the Chargers almost overtook them by scoring four touchdowns: "Let's get this thing off the ground before they score again."

❦

Clemson defensive lineman on his teammate, 320 pound William Perry: "I gave him the nickname G.E. because he's as big as a refrigerator. We were standing in an elevator in the dorm and he nearly took up the whole elevator."

🏈

Mark Gastineau, N.Y. Jets flamboyant defensive end, on the Jets play-off chances after losing to the Colts: "I'd say we've got one foot in the grave and the other on a banana peel."

🏈

Miami quarterback Dan Marino, on whether he's allowed to change the play at the line of scrimmage: "Don [Shula] says I'm always allowed to audible. As long as it works."

🏈

Fran Tarkenton, answering Frank Gifford's question on what a QB calls on third and 24: "Help!"

🏈

Mike Ditka, during a contract hassle with George Halas: "He throws nickels around as if they were manhole covers."

🏈

Gregg Pruitt, on his role as a punt-return specialist: "It's like embalming. Nobody likes it, but someone has to do it."

🏈

Jim Otto, on how it felt going one-on-one against Mean Joe Green in his prime: "You came out hurting all over, and what didn't hurt didn't work."

🏈

Dallas Cowboy running back Ron Springs, after club president, Tex Schramm, said he couldn't find holdout Randy White: "Seven figures will find him."

🏈

Billy Johnson of the Atlanta Falcons commenting on the fact that the Falcons were utilizing both he and Junior Miller at their H-back slot: "Using Junior Miller and me at the same position is like using a fastball and change-up. I'm the change-up."

🏈

Richard Byrd, rookie lineman for the Houston Oilers, explaining why he joined a group of players who shaved their heads as a sign of solidarity: "I guess it was voluntary. There were 10 guys around me, so I volunteered."

Al Denson, Wide Receiver with the Denver Broncos on what its like to know you're going to get clobbered the instant you touch a pass: "It's like walking out of a grocery store with a bag full of groceries and getting hit by a car. Sometimes you don't care what happens to the groceries."

Former Miami running back Larry Csonka, on the secret of Don Shula's self-motivation: "It's a Hungarian tradition that goes back to Attila the Hun."

Dan Connors, on the qualifications of a linebacker in the NFL: "He must have absolutely no sense of remorse."

Jack Elway, Cal State Northridge football coach, on recruiting his celebrated son, John: "I tried everything. I gave him money, let him drive my car. I even became very close with his mother. It didn't work. I still lost him to Stanford."

Pete Cronan, captain of the Washington Redskins Special Teams, on football personality: "When you step on the field, you forget everything. Like contract negotiations. That's behind you. Everything is. I like to be nice, and not just to get something. I like to treat people the way they want to be treated, because it makes life more pleasant. But I enjoy what I do on the field. I like to hit, and I hate to lose. I like the words of Woody Hayes: 'Show me a good loser and I'll show you a loser."

Sammy Baugh, when asked to compare himself with Johnny Unitas while watching Unitas during a Colt game: "I really don't know. I never saw me play."

Chapter 2

Bobby Layne, on negotiating contracts with the Chicago Bears owner-coach, George Halas: "Halas was famous for being associated with only one club all his life—the one he held over your head during salary talks."

Greg McCrary, Atlanta Falcons receiver on why he didn't go through end zone theatrics when he scored his first NFL touchdown: "One time in college I threw the ball up into the stands after a score— and they made me go up and get it."

Lynn Dickey, Green Bay quarterback, on what option he has after the coach sends in the play: "Unemployment."

With his 8th grade football team in command and about to win their big game, classy St. Paul's School (Brooklandville, MD) Middle School Coach, Mark Reuss, not wanting to embarrass their opponent by scoring again, yelled to his QB, Nolan Matthews: "No check-offs! No check-offs!"

Upon hearing this as he strolled the sideline taking pictures, Edward Brown, a witty and respected member of the English Department, known for his teaching of writing and literature, as well as his whimsical sense of humor, quipped: "Wow, what a group. They not only know football, but are familiar with Russian literature." (Anton Pavlovich Chekhov)

Russ Francis, San Francisco 49ers tight end, assessing his ability as he entered his eighth season in the NFL: "Well, I'm a fairly good surfer and an adequate sky diver."

🏈

Jack Trudeau, Illinois quarterback, explaining why when he is in a tough spot, he thinks blue: "It's relaxing ... We go into a dark room and think blue."

🏈

Ted Hendricks, Raiders defensive end on how his team would stop the Redskins tough back, John Riggins: "We'll see how far he can run with 11 guys on his back."

🏈

Marlin McKeever, USC stand-out, during a homecoming tour of the campus: "Gee, this is exciting. I've never been in one of these classrooms before!" (Kidding, of course?)

🏈

John Buchheister, football coach at Milford Mill H.S. (Md.), on how his undersized squad would stop his opponent's big backs in the state championship play-off game: "We have this guy in the 12th row behind their goal with a cannon, and when their running backs burst through he'll shoot them. It'll look like a linebacker hit them."

🏈

Cliff Stoudt, Pittsburgh quarterback, after he threw three interceptions and the Steelers turned the ball over seven times, responding to a question regarding which phase of the game he felt he'd done well at: "Tackling."

🏈

Johnny Lujack's classic reply to Frank Leahy when Army's Arnold Tucker intercepted three of his passes:
"Tucker was the only man open, Coach."

🏈

Paul Hornung, on getting married: "Never get married in the morning, because you never know who you'll meet that night."

🏈

Response by Vic Makovitch, Western Maryland College's Little All-American guard, whose odd running style prompted his coach to ask, "Didn't you ever learn how to run?": "Where I come from, we stood still and fought."

🏈

Ex-Viking player about new Minnesota coach Les Steckel, former combat Marine, whose training camp for the Vikings has been described as more of a tough boot camp: "If the Russians land in St. Paul, Steckel may win the war."

🏈

Los Angeles Raiders kicker Chris Bahr, on his position: "Place-kickers are like used cars—no one notices you until you break down."

🏈

Bill Kurtis, upon hearing allegations of drug abuse by the Chargers in 1974: "The way the Chargers played, the drug must have been formaldehyde."

🏈

Cliff Stoudt, Pittsburgh QB, asked how he would attend the Steelers Halloween party: "I may go disguised as a quarterback. Nobody will recognize me."

🏈

Ram quarterback Vince Ferragamo, commenting on the criticism he receives in L.A.: "It's not as bad as when I played with Montreal (CFL). This is paradise compared to that. They didn't even understand the game up there. Neither did I."

🏈

Raul Allegre, Baltimore Colts' placekicker, upon being congratulated by Phil Wood, WCBM Radio (Baltimore) sports reporter: "Did you think in your wildest dreams you'd be so successful so soon?": "Of course. In your wildest dreams anything can happen."

🏈

Steve Young, former 49ers' QB, after some suggested he might be a good running mate for George W. Bush: "I didn't even like backing up Joe Montana."

🏈

Edwin Simmons, Texas tailback, explaining his problems after his third arthroscopic knee surgery in eight months: "There's no pain when I'm walking, but I'm not a walking back."

🏈

Tampa Bay Buccaneer rookie linebacker Chris Washington, on why he got into karate to protect himself while growing up on the South Side of Chicago: "I was robbed twice. Once, two guys held me and set my hair on fire."

Dallas fullback Ron Springs to quarterback Danny White: "You call it, I'll haul it."

Rocky Bleier, former Pittsburgh Steelers' running back, on the aggressiveness of teammate Jack Ham: "Jack likes to hit hard, inflict a lot of pain—and that's just when he's out on a date."

Chuck Doyle, Holy Cross fullback, asked what he ran the 40 in: "Shorts."

Mike Pagel, Baltimore Colts quarterback, on coach Frank Kush's first NFL win: "It's been a lot of tough hours ... There were times he wanted to jump out of the sky. I'm just happy for him."

Joe Kapp: "I win because winning in right on, it's honest. Your blood turns sour and sticky when you lose."

Tim Foley, on which memories of his NFL career he cherishes the most: "Waking up from all my operations."

Dan Fouts, on greatness: "I know I'm not the greatest quarterback of all time. I played with him, though—Johnny Unitas. What I would like is for people to say, "There goes Dan Fouts. He won the Super Bowl. And he was part of the greatest offense in pro football history."

Joe Fields, N.Y. Jets All-Pro center: "Talent isn't talent until it shows up on the football field."

Garo Yepremian, former New Orleans Saints kicker, after deciding against a $10,000 hair transplant: "The only thing that really bothers me is that there are already so many Elvis Presley look-alikes."

●

Kenny King, on the effect of the NFL ban on stick-um: "The receivers are still making great catches, but not with their elbows."

●

Ahmed Rashad, former Vikings great receiver, on why he loves tennis: "There are no linebackers on the court."

●

Boston College wide receiver Gerard Phelan's admonition, during a false alarm, as the B.C. squad scampered down a hotel fire escape, underlining the impact quarterback Doug Flutie has had: "Women and children and Doug Flutie first."

●

Houston Oilers' quarterback, Oliver Luck: "The second team quarterback is always the most popular guy in town. You're safe as long as you don't play. When a team loses, the quarterback gets most of the criticism, whether it's justified or not."

●

Don Meredith, former Dallas quarterback on Cowboy coach Tom Landry: "He's a perfectionist. If he was married to Raquel Welch, he'd expect her to cook."

●

Jim Leonard, Tampa Bay guard, whose mother operates two homes for delinquents: "I helped her prepare for her career."

●

Jim Burt, New York Giants nose tackle, on his position: "Playing nose tackle is like going into a bar filled with your worst enemies."

Chapter 3

Karl Baldischwiler, Baltimore Colts lineman on playing surfaces: "If cows don't like to eat it, I don't want to play on it."

Roger Staubach, on why he shaved off his moustache: "People were beginning to mistake me for a kicker."

Leo Wisniewski, Baltimore Colts nose tackle, on violence: "If I thought about it, I would have to say that football is a violent sport, but it is controlled violence. The focus is not just on beating each other up."

Rocky Bleier, balding, recently retired Pittsburgh Steeler running back, ruminating on what he would like if he returned to pro ball: "I'd like the body of Jim Brown, the moves of Gale Sayers, the strength of Earl Campbell, and the acceleration of O.J. Simpson. And just once, I would like to run and feel the wind in my hair."

Reggie Williams, Cincinnati Bengal linebacker, assessing his physical talents: "Speed, strength and the ability to recognize pain immediately."

Alex Karras, on playing for George Allen: "He was great to the old guys. He had one trainer just to treat varicose veins."

Bud Winter, on his abbreviated football career at the U. of California: "The coach kept me on the team for morale purposes—I made the other players feel superior."

Joe Namath on winning: "When you win, nothing hurts."

Wilbur Young, San Diego Chargers' defensive lineman, on the toughest part of dieting off 85 pounds: "It wasn't watching what I ate. It was watching what my friends ate."

💮

Kansas State quarterback Doug Bogue, on why he changed his major from veterinary medicine to petroleum geology: "I didn't want any telephone calls at 4:00 a.m. from people saying, 'Fifi is throwing up.'"

💮

Joe Kapp, on football emotions: "Is it normal to wake up in the morning in a sweat because you can't wait to beat another human's guts out?"

💮

Norm Van Brocklin, commenting on the number of times he had to eat the ball while quarterbacking the Philadelphia Eagles when the offensive line was less that effective: "If the ball had had calories I'd have weighed three thousand pounds by the end of the year."

💮

Mike Rozier, Heisman Trophy winner, seemingly justifying receiving financial aid from alumni while a student at the University of Nebraska: "Players at Nebraska get $206 a month. I had to pay rent on my apartment, which is $260 a month. I live with my brother, so that's $130 a piece. Then there's the electric bill and the phone bill. It adds up."

💮

Ex-Chicago Bear running back Roland Harper on the importance of an offensive line: "If Walter Payton and I had run behind the Redskins offensive line, I would have had 2,000 yards a year. Walter would've had 3,000."

💮

Mark Moseley, Washington Redskins kicker, on pro kickers: "Most coaches look upon kickers the way they look upon disposable towels. They use 'em and toss 'em away."

💮

Conrad Dobler, former St. Louis Cardinal lineman reflecting on the size (6–4, 290) of former teammate Dan Dierdorff, who just retired: "Two hundred years from now, they'll dig Dan up and wonder what he was."

John Riggins, Washington Redskin running back, talking to reporters about Super Bowl preparation: "One week would be sufficient. But if there weren't two weeks, all that great journalism would go down the drain. You guys couldn't inundate your readers with all that good stuff."

Ted Hendricks, Raiders linebacker, on his dislike for lifting weight: "I lift, but only for physical appearance so I don't look bad at the beach."

Boomer Esiason, Maryland quarterback, about where he'll sign to play professional football: "I'm only 21 and I shouldn't have to make these decisions."

Dave Graf, Cleveland Brown linebacker on an ovation to teammate Dino Hall, who is 5'7": "When the crowd starting chanting, 'Dino, Dino,' his parents must have felt five feet tall."

Al Barry, Giant tackle who played in the memorable Colts-Giants play-off game in 1958, when asked about lingering football injuries: "A football injury caused me more worry the day of the championship game than it has since. I played with a smashed toe and the first thing Big Daddy Lipscomb wanted to know was, 'Which one?'"

Fran Tarkenton, on his scrambling antics: "When everything else breaks down, I don't hesitate to roam out of the pocket and do the boogaloo."

Johnny Unitas, all-time great pro quarterback, on winning: "You're a hero when you win and a bum when you lose. That's the game."

Joe Namath, reflecting on the New York Jets success: "When we won the league championship, all the married guys on the club had to thank their wives for putting up with all the stress and strain all season. I had to thank all the single broads in New York."

❧

Fran Tarkenton, former pro quarterback: "It's a lonesome walk to the sidelines, especially when thousands are cheering your replacement."

❧

Red Grange, the "Galloping Ghost" of Illinois, on competition: "I've been kicked, pummeled, spat on and cursed at, and generally abused on some of the good days I had running the ball. But somehow all this individualized attention I get from the opposition made me feel kind of proud—proud that they distinguished me as 'the guy to get.'"

❧

Henry Jordan, Green Bay tackle, about Vince Lombardi: "Yeah, he's fair. He treats us all alike—like dogs."

❧

Stan Jones, a former Chicago Bear stand-out on septuagenarian George Halas becoming more involved with the Bears: "It's like Orville Wright coming back to run United Airlines."

❧

Leon Hart, former Notre Dame great who was the Heisman Trophy winner in 1949 and All-Pro with the Detroit Lions, on present day football: "Let the coaches coach during the week and players play on Saturday. As for the pros, that's strictly big business, corporation stuff. Instead of NFL, it should be the NPSPCL—the National Push, Shove, Pass, and Catch League. I wanted to include an "H" for holding but didn't have room."

❧

Dan Hampton, Chicago defensive tackle on the Bears complicated defensive scheme: "All our defenses do, is confuse ourselves."

❧

Boomer Esiason, Maryland quarterback, on his job, one summer, as "doorman" of Joe Theismann's restaurant: "Well, yeah, bouncer, but I never had to fight anybody. Us quarterbacks can talk our way out of anything."

❧

Tony Hill, Dallas teammate of Butch Johnson, after Johnson demanded to be traded: "Butch Johnson and I have a great relationship. He has nothing to say to me and I have nothing to say to him."

John Riggins, Washington Redskins running back, characterizing a pro football player's service: "They use you until your can of gasoline is gone, and then they throw you on the junk heap."

Tim Marshall, Notre Dame tackle, upon being named to the 1983 pre-season All-American team after sitting out all of the 1982 with an injury: "If I sit out another year, I'll probably get the Heisman Trophy."

L. A. Raider Howie Long, on fans: "Fans in San Diego are lively. At L. A., everybody is worried about where they are going to get quiche in the morning."

Merlin Olsen, former L. A. Rams great, on why his old sparring partner Conrad Dobler, didn't attend Olsen's Hall of Fame Induction party: "He just didn't have the time to get his teeth filed and his claws sharpened."

Earl Campbell, regarding reporters' persistent questions about his being traded from the Houston Oilers: "You're rubbing on a bridge that's been burned. One thing about reporters: They use good English, then they twist it."

Pete Wysocki, veteran linebacker, on his 1980 New Year's resolution to do something about the monotonous "Hi Mom's" and "We're number one's," the TV viewers are subjected to: "I'm going to say hello to a cousin and claim that we're number four."

Ken de Garmo, stalwart St. Paul's School and Kansas State University linebacker, about football coaches: "I thought I knew all about hardnosed coaches until I heard about the guy who took his team in the woods and turned them loose. The ones who ran around the trees were backs and the ones who ran over the trees were linemen."

Jacob Green, Seattle Seahawk defensive end, scoffing at the statistical designation of "half-sacks": "What's that—a Baggie?"

Chapter 4

L.A. Raiders tight end Todd Christensen, on his league-leading 92 receptions: "Looks can be deceiving. They figure the white kid (Christiansen) looks slow, so maybe they can drag me down. But I've got a little funk in me."

Atlanta center Jeff Van Note on the "potential of draft choices: "Potential is a French word that means you aren't worth a damn yet."

Glenn Davis, L.A. Rams halfback after returning a kick-off 95 yards for a score, only to have an assistant coach remind him what he had done wrong: poor cuts, not following blockers, ball in wrong hand, etc.:
"But Coach, how was it for distance?"

Redskin kicker Mark Moseley on why he feels more a part of the team that most placekickers: "I speak English."

Dallas's Billy Joe DuPree, on final roster cuts in the NFL: "It's a cold business and anybody that doesn't know it is in the wrong business. You need to come in with snow shoes."

Charlie Johnson, Minnesota Viking nose tackle and defensive leader, on why the Vikes sacked John Elway five times, intercepted three passes, knocked four down, and forced three fumbles: "When you've got a young quarterback with a name and making a million dollars, you focus some attention on him."

MacArthur Lane, when a running back for the Green Bay Packers, on facing the Bears's tough linebacker, Dick Butkus: "One time he bit me. Another time he tried to break my leg, but nothing happened. I guess maybe the leg was too green."

Doug Dieken, Cleveland offensive tackle, asked how he thinks he'll be remembered: "Holding, number 73."

Doug Plank, Chicago Bear safety, on what he expected to achieve at a hearing before NFL Commissioner Pete Rozelle on his appeal of a $1,000 fine for spearing: "I hope to at least get an autographed picture."

Tom Tereshinski, Western Maryland College gridder and successful prep coach about the old days: "I can remember one hot training camp, the coach announcing, 'Okay men, today I've got some good news and some bad news. The good news is that today everybody gets a change of undergear. The bad news is: Joe, change with Mike; Mo, change with Chuck; Vic, change with ... '"

Minnesota quarterback Steve Dils on John Elway after the Broncos' quarterback had been sacked five times, intercepted three times and fumbled three times: "It must have seemed like New York at rush hour to him."

Ernie Holmes, Pittsburgh Steelers' lineman, on the Super Bowl: "We are here to play this competitional sport called football to capture the Big Iguana. We're going to get on our rubber tree and eat up all the leaves and see which one gets to the top."

Oakland Raiders' tight end Todd Christensen, on snapping the ball in punting situations: "It's like grave digging—nobody wants to do it, but somebody has to."

Fred Dryer, former L.A. Rams' defensive end, when asked if the Super Bowl is bigger than death: "No, but it comes in a bigger box."

Dallas Cowboy rookie, after proposing marriage to a girl after three dates and being asked, "Do you think you could learn to love me?" "Why not? I learned Coach Landry's signal system in only two weeks."

🏈

Lyle Alzado, L.A. Raiders' defensive lineman, on toughing it out: "If me and King Kong went into an alley, only one of us would come out. And it wouldn't be the monkey."

🏈

Leon Hart, former Notre Dame great, Heisman Trophy winner in 1949, and All-Pro with the Detroit Lions, on linemen: "A lineman's contribution to a team is equal to if not greater than that of the more glorious backs and deserves greater Heisman consideration. The line guys ought to change the rules. I once took a poll of our team to ask who was the more important—linemen or backs. The linemen won 7-4."

🏈

John Riggins, Redskin running back, when asked to recount his number one sports thrill: "Watching my neighbors' pigs being born."

🏈

A Miller Lite commercial:
Guy (Boastfully): "I was a guard for the Packers."
Girl (Incredulously): "Bill, you worked security on the parking lot."

🏈

Chicago fullback Matt Suhey, on the first pass completion of his career, a 74-yard touchdown pass to Walter Payton: "I threw one pass while at Penn State. I missed the receiver by about two days."

🏈

Kim Anderson, Baltimore Colt's defensive back, about his best friend Nesby Glasgow, recipient of the "Ed Block Courage Award": "I know how hard he hits: I'm his tackling partner. When I met him, he was 6 feet and had a full head of hair. Now he's 5-7 and losing his hair. He's paid the price for all those shots he gave. It we had a team full of him, we'd have to play in a league for midgets."

🏈

John Riggins, when asked what he thought about the Hogs, the Washington Redskin offensive line: "I think they're a bunch of slobs, but they're my kind of people."

Renaldo Nehemiah, 49er receiver, on why he is not a good practice player: "It's hard for me to wake in the morning and say I'm going to have the greatest practice I've ever had today."

Raider tight end Todd Christensen, on the Super Bowl: "It's like William Makepeace Thackeray said, 'Many win, but few make proper use of victories.' I hope to."

Dick Butkus, former Chicago Bears' linebacker, on whether he was as ornery and ferocious as everyone said he was: "I never actually set out to hurt anybody, unless it was really important—like a league game or something."

Ron Egloff, Denver Broncos' receiver, about his speed: "I have a burst of slow."

Former Cleveland Browns' great Jim Brown, on his physical condition: "Only broken-down ball players talk about people breaking their records. I am a broken-down ball player. I'm not the same man I was 20 years ago. I'm the best broken-down ball player I know."

Lynn Swann, on what kind of shape he's in since retiring from the Pittsburgh Steelers: "I'm only eight pounds heavier, but it's all in Tootsie Rolls."

Bo Jackson, Auburn running back, on his summer job as a bank teller: "The first day I was $8,000 short. Just a rookie mistake."

Matt Suhey, Chicago Bears' back, about teammate Walter Payton: "The best ground-gaining combination of all time is Walter Payton and any other running back."

Sammy Baugh on why he retired to raise cattle: "Cattle have no alumni."

Larry Lacewell, on the importance of enthusiasm in coaching: "If it meant anything at all, Tom Landry would be 0-16 every year."

David Humm, backup quarterback with the L. A. Raiders, comparing the personalities of John Madden and Tom Flores: "If Madden gives up his Lite Beer commercial, I don't think they'll get Tom to jump through the fence."

Matt Bahr, Cleveland Browns' placekicker, on competition between himself and rookie prospect, Roger Ruzek: "It's a good way to know how you're doing. I've never really heard of destructive competition."

Matt Millen, L. A. Raiders' linebacker, on when the Super Bowl victory will hit him: "When I get home and my wife tells me how we're going to spend the money."

Raider defensive lineman Howie Long after defeating Washington in the Super Bowl: "I never had hog before. It tasted good."

William Perry, Clemson middle guard, on th two year TV and post season ban imposed on the Tigers by the NCAA: "What makes it hard is that we can't watch television for two years."

Joe Greene, Steelers' defensive lineman, on why he gave up bowling: "None of the alleys would let me come back—I have an overhand delivery."

Mike Rozier, Nebraska's great running back, expressing his feelings about his offensive line after winning the Heisman Trophy: "They deserve much of the credit. If I had a chainsaw, I would cut my heart out and give it to them."

Chapter 5

Dan Dierdorf, St. Louis Cardinals' offensive lineman, announcing his intention to retire: "Ninety five percent of me is very sad that I'm retiring. But my knees are very, very happy."

Manny Fernandez, former Miami defensive lineman, taking exception to the notion that the Super Bowl seldom lives up to expectations: "What do you want us to do? Go out on the field with rockets tied to our rear ends."

Roger Staubach, announcing his retirement from pro football in Dallas: "As a quarterback I've been blessed with great receivers like Drew Pearson, Tony Hill, Billy Joe DuPree—and, of course, Herb Scott." (Herb Scott was an offensive guard who caught the final pass of Staubach's career. He caught a screen pass, out of reflex, but, of course, was an ineligible receiver.)

Tackle Ziggy Czarobski of Notre Dame, explaining to his coach, Frank Leahy, why he showers before practice: "Because it isn't so crowded at that time."

Sammy Baugh, who quarterbacked the Redskins when they were clobbered 73-0 by the Chicago Bears, asked if a sure touchdown pass dropped by Washington would have changed the outcome of the game: "Sure it would have. The score would have been seventy-three to seven."

Charlie Waters, Dallas Cowboys, on why Aaron Mitchell is called A.M.–P.M.: "Because they're wide awake when he hits 'em and their lights are out when he walks away."

Sonny Jurgenson, former Redskins' quarterback, describing what he looked like when he ran the ball: "When I run from the pocket, I look like a crane with a broken leg."

Cliff Stoudt, Birmingham Stallions (USFL) quarterback, [by way of the Steelers] after the Stallions playoff loss to the Philadelphia Wranglers: "I just have an empty feeling. I've been playing for 50 weeks, and there's nothing to do tomorrow."

Alex Karras, on his tenure at Iowa: "I played at Iowa for only two terms—Truman's and Eisenhower's."

Doug Buffone, Chicago Bears' linebacker, on Fran Tarkenton's retirement: "I haven't hit him yet and now I never will."

John Riggins, on Dallas coach Tom Landry's view that inferior teams can win the Super Bowl: "If I had all the talent and couldn't win it. I guess I'd have to think of something to say too."

Jack Lambert, Steelers' linebacker, expressing his views with 'bumper stickers': "Caution: I don't break for liberals."
—and—
"Guns cause crime like flies cause garbage."

Los Angeles Express lineman, Jeff Hart, a former starter for the Indianapolis (nee Baltimore) Colts, on get-acquainted parties with his new teammates: "If the quarterbacks are buying, it's steak and lobster. If we're (offensive linemen) buying, it's pizza and beer."

Alvin Garrett, Washington Redskins' receiver, who is a native Texan, commenting on the Washington-Dallas Cowboys' rivalry: "Down in Texas, the Redskins are known as Russia's team."

Jack Kemp on winning: "Winning is like shaving. You do it every-day or you look like a bum.

🏈

Great quarterback Sammy Baugh, as his career went on and on, and his aging bones felt the pounding of the years, on being asked if this might be his last year: "I don't know. Maybe last year was."

🏈

Joe Theismann, Redskin quarterback, about the booing he received from Washington frans during the Giants game: "Washington fans are still the greatest. Boo? I didn't hear any boos. Well, all right, but it was more like a hum, wasn't it? They're still the greatest."

🏈

Earl Campbell, Houston running back, on how it felt to be one of the NFL's most productive backs on the least productive team: "It hurts, it's got to hurt. But I try to tell myself it's not the guy who wins the race who gets respect, but the guy who never quits trying and keeps coming."

🏈

David Archer, quarterback for 2-3 Iowa State: "If we don't get the killer instinct, somebody is going to get killed."

🏈

Raymond Berry, former Baltimore Colt great, about the Colts leg-endary 1958 team: "If I had a surplus million or two, I'd get 'em all together, rent a boat and take 'em on a cruise."

🏈

Cliff Stoudt, during the 1983 season, after a mediocre perform-ance with the Steelers: "Was it frustrating? No, all those years sitting on the bench, that was frustrating. This is embarrassing. I guess I'd rather be frustrated than embarrassed."

🏈

Cliff Stoudt, asked what he was going to do after his "embarrass-ing" performance: "I guess I'll go home, watch the replay on my tape machine and boo myself."

🏈

John Riggins, Redskin running back on his reputation for being out of sync with the rest of the world: "I don't know if I'm ahead or behind, but I know I'm not even."

Mark Moseley, Redskin placekicker, on how he feels about his Super Bowl ring: "It may end up in the gutter, but if it does, I'll be wearing it."

William Perry, Clemson lineman who weights 320 pounds: "Even when I was little, I was big."

Ordell Braase, Colts' defensive end from South Dakota State, on small college players making the pros: "Well, it's better to be in the rear and discovered than up front and found out."

Terry Bradshaw, Steeler quarterback, asked at a luncheon if he was still involved in any way with estranged wife Jo Jo Starbuck: "Just financially."

Tampa Bay defensive end Brad Culpepper to teammate Chidi Ahanotic after the latter got a 15-yard penalty and a $2,500 fine for his sack dance over Atlanta Falcons' quarterback Chris Chandler: "They didn't call you for taunting. They called you for bad dancing."

Bubba Smith, when asked how he could be so aggressively hostile on the football field, yet always managed to show a smile at breakfast: "That's easy. I go to bed with a coat hangar in my mouth."

Sheldon Nelson, Towson State (Md.) defensive tackle, on defense: "My old Marine Corps coach once said: 'God is on the side of the team with the best defensive line.' Going to Liberty Baptist, I kind of wondered, but after we won (13-3), I figure he was right."

John Riggins, Redskin running back on whether he was worried about going into a game because so much was expected of him: "I was camping out one night with an old fella named Glenn Jenkins back in Centralia, Kansas, and I could hear the coyotes howling, and they sounded like they were getting mightly close. I asked Glenn if he felt nervous. He said, 'I've probably killed 200 of them. It doesn't exactly raise the hair on the back of my neck.' It's like NFL games. I've probably gone through 130 of them, and they don't exactly raise the hair on the back of my neck."

Willie Gault, Chicago's rookie receiver and world-class sprinter, when asked if defensive players try to intimidate him: "No, mostly I get congratulations about Helsinki. Besides, I don't stick around very long."

Bob Kasel, on Baylor's 29-year-old U.S. Army veteran, Ray Gibbons, who plays tackle and is 6-7 and 305 lbs.: "He may not be much of a football player, but he'll sure come in handy when the Russians invade Waco."

Todd Blackledge, former Penn State quarterback, after calling his parents to tell them about his lucrative contract with the Kansas City Chiefs: "I told them it was the last collect call I'd ever make."

John Riggins, on his doubts about retiring: "My big fear is where I'm going to find another job with a six month vacation."

Chapter 6

Garry Green, Kansas City Chiefs' cornerback, on the new fine system introduced by Coach John Mackovic for such infractions as kneeling or sitting on a helmet, etc.: "It's not kindergarten, but maybe it's high school at times."

❧

Mike Rozier, Nebraska tailback on Big Eight and All American rival Marcus Dupree of Oklahoma: "I know the guy down the street says he's going to win the Heisman Trophy. But he's kind of young and really doesn't know what he's talking about."

❧

Los Angeles Raider Ted Hendricks on how he has managed not to miss a game since the 10th grade: "I keep my cleats out of the turf, my head on a swivel, and stay away from pile-ups."

❧

Scott Bacigalupo, St. Paul's School QB on their 1989 championship team, jesting with a reporter who asked: "Last year at this time you had passed for two touchdowns and this season you already have seven. What's the difference?"
Bacigalupo: "Five."

❧

Ordell Braase, former Baltimore great defensive end, describing one of his former teammates: "He was like a tea bag. You never knew his strength until he was in hot water."

❧

Joe Theismann, Redskin quarterback, on football expectations in Dallas: "They had the second-best record, yet they're not burying the Cowboys with shovels. They're burying them with bulldozers."

❧

Neal Olkewicz, Redskin linebacker, on why the Washington defense does not have a colorful nickname like "Doomsday" or "Steel Curtain": "Because if things start going bad, people start going after the guys with the nicknames first."

Bob Chandler, NBC analyst, on why his former teammate at Buffalo, O. J. Simpson, did not block: "He had to have the feeling that no one could touch him."

Mike Flynn, student at Richard Todd's football camp, when it was announced that Todd would "demonstrate what he does best": "What's that? Throw interceptions."

Jim Dickey, on the motivational advantage of having six new 160-foot light poles on a field that often has winds over 90 miles an hour: "The first player who drops a pass, fumbles, or misses a tackle has to go up and change a light bulb."

Freshman quarterback in a dialogue with his coach, as to why he called a different pass play than that called for by the coach, which went for the winning touchdown:

QB: "I had a feeling. I looked at our halfback; his number was 42. Then I looked at our fullback; his number was 21. So I called 62."

Coach: "But that adds up to 63."

QB: Yeah, but if I was as smart as you, we wouldn't have won the game."

Jim Ringo, on how it feels to be tackled by Laurence Taylor of the New York Giants: "Next morning you go to workmen's compensation to apply for 70% disability."

Bill Raferty, after being told by his high school coach to go out and have a lot of fun, and then losing a game by 35 points: "That was the worst fun I ever had."

Charlie Jackson of the old Chicago Cardinals, recalling what it was like for a defensive back to meet the fabled Jimmy Brown after he had broken through the line and built momentum: "It's an awful sensation when Brown comes blowin' through the hole and right at you. You feel like you're trapped on a trestle by an unscheduled freight train."

Dolphin wide receiver, Nat Moore, on why his 11th season definitely will be his last: "So my body can enjoy the money it's earned."

Russ Francis, San Francisco's tight end and all-around daredevil finally yielding to Coach Bill Walsh's request that he not race an experimental plane because there would be lengthy rehabilitation time if he were to get injured: "I told Bill that I would be flying 50 feet above the ground at 300 mph. If anything went wrong, we wouldn't be concerned about rehabilitation."

Roger Staubach, former Dallas quarterback, who never got to call his own plays in the huddle, after a faltering start on a football banquet speech: "I keep waiting for Mike Ditka or Bill Truax to bring in the words."

Charlie Waters, Dallas defensive back, after watching a computerized game that matched the 1971 Cowboys against a team of all-time greats including the great Jim Thorpe: "For an 84 year old Indian, he showed me some great moves."

Mike Curtis, former Baltimore Colt linebacker: "The 'breakfast of Champions' is not a cereal. It's the opponent."

Sid Luckman, former Chicago Bear great quarterback, commenting on the modern-day version: "The Bears aren't dead; they just don't want to get involved."

Terry Bradshaw, Pittsburgh quarterback, on how he tried to ease the tension on his placekicker, Matt Bahr, when they were tied with just nine seconds left in the overtime period against the Browns: "I tried not to put any pressure on him. I said, 'Miss it and you're cut.'"

Jay Hilgenberg, Chicago Bear center, on how his father had taught him and his two brothers to make the long snap: "We were the only family that ever went out and played catch with our backs to each other."

In 1976, tackle Jim Parker and Coach Ewbank represented the Colts at rededication cermonies at Yankee Stadium. Parker commented: "Fifty five thousand people stood up and booed us like hell. Great. They remembered us."

John Riggins, Redskin running back, on why he plays the game: "I play the game for the fun, for the moment. And, the cash."

Carl Mauck, Houston Oiler center, hearing the news that one of the team's linemen will receive a 25-pound assortment of steaks and sausages after every game in which Earl Campbell rushes for 100 yards: "Can they work out something to get us some gas."

Brent Ziegler, Syracuse fullback, upon hearing that he was the 265th selection in the NFL draft: "I think they drafted in alphabetical order."

Ronnie Lott, San Francisco All-Pro-Cornerback, on why he won't report until he signs for what is believed to be near $800,000 a season: "I know what I am worth to the 49-ers, but if I get hurt before I get a new contract, people will constantly remind me how close I came to making some big money."

Cliff Stoudt, the former Steelers' quarterback, listing one of his favorite charities: "Defensive backs. Some guys give to the United Fund. Me? I give to Denver defensive backs."

Brian Blados, North Carolina tackle and first round draft choice of the Cincinnati Bengals, to reporters who seemed preoccupied with his 6'4½", 295-pound frame: "You guys measuring me for a suit or something."

Herkie Walls, 5-foot-8, 154 pound receiver/returner from Houston, who runs the 40 in 4.4, asked if he'd be able to withstand the punishment in the NFL: "People have got to catch me first."

Bob Henko, Tampa Bay Buccaneer reserve quarterback, kidding about the playboy image of former University of Florida teammate Chris Collingsworth, now with the Cincinnati Bengals: "We call him Don Juan. The girls Don Juan him."

Mark Murphy, Redskins' safety describing how to defense Eric Dickinson, the Rams nifty running back: "With him, you have to be intelligent in your pursuit. You have to surround him, so that no matter which was he goes you have someone to cut him off at the pass."

Mike Curtis, former Baltimore linebacker, on why he tackled a fan who had run onto the field and grabbed the football: "He was in my territory. He didn't belong there. He was also stealing 20 dollars— that's how much the balls cost."

John Unitas, pro football's greatest quarterback, acknowledging that today's players are different—bigger, faster, and smarter. But are they better: "No, expansion has diluted the talent, and lots of guys are here today who wouldn't have been signed seven or eight years ago. And they don't have the dedication, the desire, and the drive that we had. As long as they make the team and get their money, they don't care what happens. Winning isn't that important to them. They won't spend the time and effort to make themselves better. They're not willing to sacrifice. They don't have the right attitude."

Don Smith, Atlanta Falcons' defensive end, on the expected return of fellow defensive end Jeff Yeates for a 13th NFL season: "The thing that's kept Jeff around is his longevity."

Chapter 7

Jack Rothrock, who played center for Guilford College in its 60-6 loss to Bear Bryant's Maryland team in 1945: "The crowd sang 'Maryland, My Maryland' after each touchdown, even on the four that were called back. By the end of the first quarter, I knew all the words."

Earl Campbell, Houston Oilers' running back, philosophizing: "You have always got to strive in life. Death's only an arm's length away. And my arm's not that long."

Napoleon McCallum, Navy's outstanding halfback and 1984 Heisman Trophy candidate explaining to writer Bill Glauber how he can to terms with his desire to play pro football on one hand, and his military commitment, on the other: "I had no choice. I just had to find peace within myself. I'm glad I'm settled with myself. I'm OK. I'm not screaming about it and I'm not looking for ways to get out anymore. Living at the Naval Academy has taught me that you can do anything you put your mind to and you can do it quickly. It has taught me how to deal with people and it has taught me that moms and dads are really important. And it has also taught me that you best friend is really yourself. You can't let yourself down."

Jeff Bostic, Redskin center: "When someone calls you a Hog in the Washington area, it's like being called the First Lady."

Reggie Kinlaw, Raider nose guard who did terrible things to Bostic in the 1984 Super Bowl: " He sure played like the First Lady."

Don Kindt, on attending the Chicago Bears camp at St. Joseph's College (IN) in the 40's and 50's: "I spent so much time there I thought I was going to be ordained."

Mike Rentko, old time stalwart gridder at Newport Township High School (Pa.) and Western Maryland College, on the tough old days: "One time we were playing this team that was so dirty, on just about every play their center would bite me. So I asked the referee what I should do about it. 'Well,' he snapped, 'the only thing I advise is that you play him only on Fridays.'"

Lynn Swann, Pittsburgh Steelers' nifty receiver, watching Terry Bradshaw stagger to his feet after being run over by a herd of blitzers: "Nice going, Terry, that's the way to pick up those linebackers."

Joe Gardi, N.Y. Jets' defensive coach, when it was mentioned that setting up defenses against the high scoring San Diego Chargers was like playing a chess game: "I hope not. I'm a pinochle man."

Alex Karras on kickers: "Placekickers aren't football players. They're hired feet."

Mark Gastineau, Jets' defensive end, after holding a football clinic at the Rikers Island (N.Y.) jail: "Three guys asked me to show them how to run out for a 250-yard pass."

Doug Flutie, Boston College quarterback, on the size of the Notre Dame team he was about to face: "Were they huge? Oh, what an understatement! I got a creak in my neck looking up at them."

Frank Gifford, former all-pro player and noted broadcaster: "Pro football is like nuclear warfare. There are no winners, only survivors."

Matt Millen, Raider linebacker, upon hearing that Russ Grimm of the Redskins said he'd run over his mother to win the Super Bowl: "I'd run over his mother, too."

*

Dan Goldstein, on why the City College (N. Y.) football team didn't score a point in 1945: "We kept tipping off our plays. Every time we broke the huddle, three backs would be smiling and the fourth would be pale as a ghost."

*

A.J. Duhe, Miami Dolphins' linebacker, after his fifth operation in the last 18 months: "The next time I see a doctor, it better be for an autopsy."

*

Joe Ferguson, 39 year-old Tampa Bay Buccaneers' quarterback, who was named one of America's sexiest men: "My wife hasn't said too much about it—since she stopped rolling on the floor laughing."

*

Mickey Holmes, following Miami's 27-10 victory over Notre Dame: "If Miami is not ranked ahead of Notre Dame, then AP should move their headquarters to the Vatican."

*

Arkie Willson, about the Raiders' 270 lb. Offensive linemen, Curt Marsh and Henry Lawrence: "They're so tough they warm up by playing catch with the field house."

*

University of Virginia receiver Herman Moore, describing the Cavaliers Atlantic Coast Conference title chances: "We're not only in the driver's seat—it's our car."

*

Seattle Seahawks' wide receiver Steve Largent trying to explain his team's 4-8 record: "For the longest time, people have said what the Seattle Seahawks need to do is play consistently. We're playing consistently."

*

Chicago's defensive lineman Dan Hampton after the Bears exploded for 28 points in the fourth quarter to beat the Minnesota Vikings: "It smells like napalm around here."

*

Ali Haji-Sheikh, Washington Redskins' field goal kicker about his job: "Kicking is 95 percent boredom and 5 percent sheer terror."

🏈

Babe Laufenberg, journeyman QB, on his battle to hang on with the Dallas Cowboys: "I'll do anything Coach Jimmy Johnson wants me to do. If he wants me to run 26 miles through the hills, I'll do it. If he wants me to carry the water bottles, I'll do it. If he wants me to go to his barber and get my hair cut like him—well, you have to draw the line somewhere."

🏈

Tony Mandarich, after joining the Green Bay Packers: "I'm happy to be a Packer. I did call Green Bay a village in *Playboy,* but every village needs a village idiot."

🏈

Dallas Cowboys' offensive guard Nate "The Kitchen" Newton on his weight problem: "Every night, I tell myself: 'I'm gonna dream about my girl. I'm gonna dream about my girl.' But it's always ham hocks."

🏈

John Unitas, the greatest quarterback the NFL has ever known, commenting on his days with the Bloomington Rams, a semi-pro team: "We didn't have a team bus. We had a team bike."

🏈

Doug Williams, Redskins' quarterback, on whether he would wear gloves to combat the cold in their game against Chicago: "I'll practice in them. But in the game I'll do it like Smith-Barney, the old way."

🏈

Matt Suhey and Walter Payton on their Alaskan hunting trip: *Suhey,* awakening in their tent one night: "Why are you putting on running shoes?"
Payton: "There's a bear outside."
Suhey: "You can't outrun the bear."
Payton: "I don't have to outrun him. All I have to do is outrun you."

🏈

Lester Hayes, L. A. Raiders' cornerback, after playing against the Eagles' scrambling quarterback Randall Cunningham: "He must shower in Vaseline."

Football player, injured on field, to teammate: "That was the Statue of Liberty play all right. I got creamed by the huddled masses."

Seattle offensive guard Bryan Millard on the toughness of Seahawks' linebacker Fredd Young: "I'd rather sandpaper a bobcat's butt in a phone booth than be tackled by Fredd."

Howie Long, defensive end for L. A. Raiders, on Bo Jackson: "If Bo and I were both stallions, I think I could command—based on physical characteristics and past performances—a stud fee of maybe $500,000. Bo would get $5 million. It's like Bo's Secretariat and I'm Mr. Ed."

Billy Joe Tolliver, rookie quarterback of the San Diego Chargers, about the first time his parents took him to the big city of Fort Worth, Texas: "We go into this big, old store and Dad tells Ma, 'Just go and look around. We'll just wait here for you.' So we're sitting in the lobby and I look down the hall and there's these two big silver doors. I asked my dad, 'What are those down there?' He said, 'I don't know, let's go look at it.' Me and Pop are standing there checking out these doors, and all of a sudden they just open up. We're amazed. And this lady walks up, and she has to be the homeliest woman I've ever seen. She walked inside those doors into that little closet there. All of a sudden they closed up and I looked up and I see these numbers flashing: two, three, four, five, six, and it stops. I'm looking at my dad and he's looking at numbers and they go: five, four, three, two, one, and the doors open and the best-looking woman you've ever seen in your life steps out of there. I said, 'Pop, how'd that happen?' He said, 'I don't know, boy, but you need to get your momma. We'll run her through it a couple of times.'"

Kansas City Chiefs offensive tackle, John Tait, after lumbering 28 yards with a lateral from QB Trent Green to set up a winning field goal against Cleveland: "Well, I've got to give credit to my offensive line ..."

Chapter 8

Stan Waldemore, after watching Jet teammate Greg Bingham get knocked high in the air, turn over slowly, and fall to the turf: "It was a lousy block, but Greg had great hang time."

Jack Kemp, on why pro football is a great training ground for politics: "It prepares you for booing, cheering, and being cut, sold, traded, or hanged in effigy."

Giants' lineman Garry Reasons, after teammate Jim Burt had recovered a fumble in mid-air and waddled 39 yards for a T.D.: "I was lying there watching him and I was afraid he might trip over a yard line."

Nick Lowery, 41 year old kicker, after being released by the N.Y. Jets: "I'm not really a free agent, but I'm very affordable."

Trace Liggett, Kansas University lineman who is 6'4" and 285 lbs., when asked his time in the 40-yd. dash: "I really don't know. I do know though that they used as a sun dial to time me."

Former San Francisco 49ers' tackle Bob St. Clair, a recent Pro Football Hall of Fame inductee, when asked if players of his era could play today: "The question isn't whether we could play today. The question is whether today's player could play in our era."

Texas A&M cornerback Chet Brooks following his team's lose to Ohio State in the Cotton Bowl on Jan. 1, 1987: "It's like eating squash. It doesn't go down very well, but it goes down sooner or later."

Steve Bartkowski about the difference playing behind the L. A. Rams' line after years with the Falcons: "Football seems so different from an upright position."

George Martin, N.Y. Giants' 255 lb. defensive lineman, on his 78 yd. touchdown run after intercepting a pass by DenverQB John Elway: "When I caught the ball, it was bright sunny day. By the time I got to the end zone, it was partly cloudy."

Jim Thorpe on money: "They say that money talks. The only thing it ever said to me was 'good-bye!'"

Tampa Buccaneer guard Sean Farrell's response to a heckling fan: "Look, why don't we talk about this Monday when you pick up my trash?"

Phil Simms, Giant QB, kidding teammate Jim Burt: "If we didn't have a huddle, Jim would have no social life."

New York Jets back-up QB Pat Ryan, when asked if he had been discouraged by all the time he spent on the bench: "I'd rather be discouraged than out in the real world."

Lyle Alzado, on his college football coach: "He was so chintzy, he didn't show game movies; he showed slides."

Liberty University football player Barry Rice, on how Gospel and gridiron co-exist at the Baptist school: "If Jesus were a football player, he'd play fair, he'd play clean and he'd put the guy across the line on his butt."

Steve Wallace of San Francisco on the possibility of the 49ers repeating as Super Bowl Champions: "We want to be like Rudolph the Red-Nosed Reindeer and go down in history."

Doug Sutherland, ex-Minnesota Viking, on what kind of equipment you needed to wear against Conrad Dobler, who had a reputation as a dirty player: "A string of garlic around your neck and a wooden stake."

Cleveland Browns' punter Bryan Wagner on his club-record 91 punts in '89: "It's a shankless job."

Karl Nelson of the New York Giants, after he retired and indicated he wasn't interested in going into coaching: "General Manager George Young said I was too well-adjusted to be a coach."

Gilman School (Baltimore, MD) football Coach Sherm Bristow, after his team scored on a second half kick-off when his returner fumbled on his 35, the ball came to rest in a massive puddle, and a teammate picked it up and raced down the sideline for a TD: "We set that play up at halftime."

Former Duke QB Ben Bennett, after playing in his first Arena Football game: "The game looks like your VCR is stuck on search."

Cornerback Tim McKyer, on the difference between the facilities of his new team, the Dolphins and his former team, the 49ers: "I've definitely got something to get used to. I left a Cadillac and now I'm a Chevy."

Lou Groza, great Cleveland Browns' placekicker, on the derivation of his nickname "The Toe": "The press had a choice—the Toe or the Heel—and I won."

Cincinnati Bengals' left-handed quarterback, Boomer Esiason: "Dan Marino has the greatest right arm in football."

St. Louis (now Arizona) Cardinals' Neal Lomax bout the long time it took the replay officials to decide if a ball had been caught in-bounds or out-of-bounds: "I thought they were ordering a pizza."

The Los Angeles Raiders' Bob Golic on the nature of his position: "If you're mad at your kid, you can either raise him to be a nose tack-le or send him out to play in the freeway. It's all about the same."

Tackle Mike Schad of the Eagles when they were in London to play the Cleveland Browns: "I hope to visit the Tower of London. I want to see the torture chambers. I'm sure Buddy's (Coach Buddy Ryan) been there already."

Russ Francis, New England Patriots' tight end on defensive line-men: "If their IQ's were five points lower, they would be geraniums."

Former Kansas City Chiefs' tight end Fred Arbanas, who is blind in one eye, when asked by an official what he would do if he lost his good eye: "I'd be an official just like you."

Frank Cornish, the U.C.L.A. All-American center, who is 6'4 ?" and 265 lbs., wanted to be a jockey when he was a youngster. His mother, Gloria, talked him out of it: "I told him, 'Son, you are the size of the average jockey now ... and you're 4 years old.'"

Former Arena Football league quarterback Ben Bennett, hired by the Chicago Bears, two of whose three regular QB's were injured: "I guess you could refer to me as worst-case scenario."

Gordon King, on how it feels to line up against 6'9", 280 lb. Too Tall Jones: "How would you feel if you had to look a guy straight in the belly button?"

Trevor Matich, BYU center who snapped the ball to Marc Wilson, Jim McMahon, and Steve Young: "If their hands were worth $60,000,000 to the pros, I wonder what my rear end will go for?"

❡

Andre Rison, Indianspolis Colts' receiver from Michigan State on his $890,000 signing bonus, half of which was deferred: "My money is sleeping. I hope when it wakes up, there's more of it."

❡

Mike Pagel, following an Akron (Ohio) Beacon Journal telephone survey asking who should be the Cleveland Browns' quarterback and he got 704 votes to Bernie Kosar's 94: "I'm sure glad I got through 702 times, and I appreciate the other two people calling, whoever they are."

❡

Harmon Wages, former Altanta Falcons' back and TV sportscaster, on his new radio talk show: "My mama always said I had a face for radio."

❡

Veteran Denver Bronco defender Karl Mecklenburg, on his progress: "From nose guard to defensive end to inside linebacker to outside linebacker. I'm moving right up the evolutionary ladder."

❡

Dan Hampton of the Chicago Bears, explaining how the Tampa Bay Buccaneers beat the Minnesota Vikings late in the 1990 season: "It's the combination of two factors, Tampa having new life with a coaching change and Minnesota checking flight schedules to the Bahamas."

❡

Tunch Ilkin, Steelers' tackle, on the benefits derived from the team going four weeks without scoring a touchdown: "We never had to practice kicking off."

❡

Dick Butkus, explaining his life-time achievement awards from two Chicago hospitals: "Why not? I used to fill the beds with running backs every Sunday."

Chapter 9

Joe Namath, former pro QB and NBC sports analyst, commenting about NBC's Thanksgiving game featuring two struggling teams (Detroit and Denver): "It should be a pretty good game—even though they're both playing like turkeys."

Jimmy Williams, Lions's linebacker, on why he always shoots for the moon: "Because I know that even if I fall short, I'll land among the stars."

St. Louis All-Pro receiver Roy Green, held to one catch in a 27-17 loss to the N.Y. Giants, assessing the Cardinal day: "When all was said and done for us, more was said than done."

Mike Reid, football player turned concert pianist: "There are a thousand reasons for failure, but not a single excuse."

Howie Long, L. A. Raiders' defensive end, on what it is like to have running back Bo Jackson in the line-up: "Ever been in a Porsche when the turbo kicks in?"

Deion Sanders, Dallas Cowboys' defensive back, when asked to speculate on his team's chances of making the playoffs: "I think you need Dionne Warwick, not Deion Sanders."

Observation of a player on the sideline when a teammate streaked down field, went by the defender, and then dropped a perfectly thrown 50-yard pass from his QB: "Coach, he must have heard footprints."

Andre Ware's response to Bob Hope at the A.P. All-American presentations on the Hope show:
Hope: "I hope you're a great success, Andre."
Ware: "The same to you, Mr. Hope."

🏈

Kim Cunningham, on why Lyle Alzado rejoined the Raiders at age 41 after four years of retirement: "He was seeking repentance for the three movies he had made: *Lapped Again, Club Fed,* and *Hang Fire.*"

🏈

Chicago Bears' defensive tackle Steve McMichael, comparing quarterbacks: "I'd go so far as to say Randall Cunningham [of the Eagles] is the best athlete in NFL history to play that position. I'd much rather play against an old guy like Joe Montana. He goes down when you breathe on him."

🏈

Howie Long, Los Angeles Raiders' lineman on whether the NFL team is moving to Oakland: "I don't know. Al Davis' operation is as leak-proof as Jacques Cousteau's submarine."

🏈

Harry Pollock, outstanding gridder at St. Paul's School (Brooklandville, Md.), describing his fleet-footed teammate, halfback Hank Smith: "Could he run? Are you kidding? He had more moves than the Mayflower Van Lines."

🏈

The late Harold "Red" Grange telling the story about his legendary No. 77: "The guy in front of me got 76, the guy in back got 78."

🏈

"Snake" Stabler, former great QB with the Raiders now a TV analyst, describing a punishing run over a cornerback by Kansas City's 250 lb. Christian Okaye: "That was like a pick-up truck running over a rooster."

🏈

LeRoy Merritt, amiable old-time Western Marylander gridder and successful Maryland businessman, offering a whimsical view as to why an Art Course might help football players: "Well, they might run a draw play with greater proficiency."

Section II:
The Coaches

Chapter 10

Wade Phillips, on replacing Buffalo Bills' Marv Levy, who holds a Master's Degree from Harvard: "Marv's more likely to quote Homer and I'm more likely to quote Homer Simpson."

Mike Rentko, Associate Head coach , St. Paul's School, Brookland-ville, Md., when asked about the ideal lineman: "It would have to be King Kong. He was coordinated and could climb buildings and swat things out of the air at the same time."

University of Maryland line coach Elliot Uzelac, complimenting his guard, Jamie Wu, who weighed 320 pounds, but cut down on heavy eating to slim down and gain more speed: "He was going to burp his way through life."

John Mackovic, former Kansas City coach, who feels pro athletes are different than they used to be, cites the following changes in the way coaches have addressed their players over the years:
"Go over and stand in the corner."
"Please stand in the corner."
"How about if you went over and stood in the corner."
"How about us talking about you standing in the corner."
"Why don't I go over and stand in the corner for you."

Bear Bryant, upon receiving an honorary degree: "For a person who didn't take advantage of his scholarship to get an education, this is like getting a battlefield commission."

Ray Jenkins, one-time Montana State football coach, discussing his team's chances for the forthcoming season: "We definitely will be improved this year. Last year we lost 10 games. This year we only scheduled nine."

Dana X. Bible, Texas A&M coach, delivering the quietest, shortest, and perhaps the most effective half-time talk after his team had played poorly in the first half and the scoreboard reflected it: "Well, girls, shall we go?"

Steve Spurrier, Florida coach, telling fans that a fire at Auburn's football dorm had destroyed 20 books: "But the real tragedy was that 15 hadn't been colored in yet."

Bum Phillips, on playing in Pittsburgh in December: "In that kind of weather you don't have to practice to be miserable."

Jack Molesworth, Western Maryland College (Westminster, Md.) football coach upon learning of Michigan's annual football budget: "With that kind of a budget, I could invade Albania."

Rick Venturi, Northwestern football coach, after losing to Ohio State, 63–20: "The only difference between me and General Custer is that I have to watch the films."

Cardinals' Dave McGinnis, on the problems of rookie defensive end Mao Tosi: "He found out it's way different out in the pasture than when you get in the pen with the bull."

Tom Landry, Dallas Cowboys' coach on 12th-round pick, sprinter Carl Lewis: "We'd need two quarterbacks—one to make the first throw and the other to relay it to him (Lewis) downfield."

Duke head coach Steve Sloan, on preparing his team to play against 6 foot-3, 320 pound middle guard William Perry of Clemson: "To resemble William Perry, we are going to rent a Winnebago for our offensive line to practice against. In William Perry, Clemson has two of the finest middle guards in the country."

🏈

John Ralston, asked what advice he would offer his successor, Red Miller, after being fired by the Broncos: "I'm leaving behind three envelopes. They are marked One, Two, and Three.

If he loses three in a row, he is to open Envelope One, in which he will find a three-word message—'Blame your Predecessor.'

If he loses three more in a row, he is to open Envelope Two, in which he will find another three-word message—'Blame your Quarterback.'

If he loses three more in a row, he is to open Envelope Three, in which he will find one more three-word message—'Prepare Three Envelopes!'"

🏈

Les Steckel, the Vietnam veteran who replaced Bud Grant as the Minnesota Vikings coach, on maturity and experience: "I know I'm young and following the legend of Bud Grant, but I've led 210 Marines and 80 Vietnamese soldiers into combat, so don't talk to me about being a head coach."

🏈

Hank Stram, former NFL coach, on running backs who try to leap over tacklers: "One of these days a back's going to jump in the air, two guys are going to grab him, each by a leg and make a wish, and that back's going to be in trouble."

🏈

George Welsh, former Navy coach, and later at Virginia, on playing before huge crowds: "Our teams at Navy used to like playing in places like Michigan where there were 100,000 people watching. We didn't win any, but the players enjoyed the trips."

🏈

Lee Corso, analyst during the Maryland-Tennessee game in the Citrus Bowl: "There's an interesting story about Maryland's tight end Bill Rogers. He transferred from the Naval Academy. Boy, that's like defecting."

Syracuse Coach Dick Mac Pherson, asked how good Nebraska was following the Cornhuskers win over his team 63-7: "Well, they're not the best team I've ever seen. The Pittsburgh Steelers are pretty good."

Wendell Mosely, Texas Southern football coach, describing his team's trouncing by Grambling: "Grambling was 14 points ahead before I could get my headset on."

Mike McCormack while Baltimore Colts' coach on statistics: "Statistics are like a loose woman. You can do anything you want with them."

John Bridgers, personable coach who elevated the football program at Johns Hopkins and then spent some years with the Baltimore Colts and at other colleges and later became Athletic Director at Florida State, on what he wanted most out of coaching: "When I was young I wanted to be the best coach in the nation. Later I just wanted to be the oldest."

George Halas, on why the modern football player is so much tougher to handle than the old-timer: "Ask a modern player to drive his head through a brick wall and right away he'll ask you 'Why?'"

Mike McCormack, while coach of the Baltimore Colts, about his players: "I'll take my guys with the 5.0 speed and the 4.6 hearts and beat your guys with the 4.5 speed and 5.0 hearts."

Pat Dye, Auburn coach, on his basic football philosphy: "I like throwing the football and I like all that fancy stuff, but I'm going to be honest with you—I like it jaw-to-jaw and in the trenches."

Craig Morton, on his coaching debut with the Denver Gold, a 21-19 win over the Birmingham Stallions, when asked if the experience had been less taxing that playing in the NFL: "Are you kidding me? I have a sore throat, my knees ache and by back hurts."

Chuck Mills, on his U.S. Merchant Marine football team's clobbering by Bucknell, 37-0: "Fortunately, we were really up for the game. Otherwise, they'd have killed us."

Woody Hayes, the long-time Ohio State coach on football's fickle fans: "They'll give you the new Cadillac one year and the next year they give you the gas to get out of town."

Sam Rutigliano on Cleveland's 9-7 (1983) season: "We have the makings of a very good team and it's time for us to reload, not rebuild."

Frank Leahy, Notre Dame's great football coach, on criticism: "Criticism is like money: you shouldn't worry about it, but you should worry over the lack of it."

Steve Owen, former Giants' coach, on nostalgia: "The older you get, the faster you ran as a kid."

Vince Lombardi, as he crawled wearily into bed after long trip and his wife commented, "God, your feet are cold!": "Here at home, you can call me Vince."

Mike Rentko, Associate Head Coach, St. Paul's School (Brooklandville, Md.), on his definition of what makes a successful coach: "A good coach is one who can be chased down the street by irate alumni and make it look like he's leading a parade."

Frank Howard, Clemson coach, on how his team managed to upset a much larger, much heavier Texas Christian team in the 1960 Bluebonnet Bowl: "Those other boys were so big they tilted the field and we were able to play downhill all the way."

Chapter 11

Tom Landry on being congratulated for being the only coach in Dallas Cowboy history: "All it means is that I haven't had a promotion in 21 years."

◉

Sam Rutigliano, of the Cleveland Browns, on the divine power of Al Davis: "He knows the serial number of the Unknown Soldier."

◉

Joe Paterno, Penn State coach on why honorable recruiting is important: "Recruiting is like courting your wife. After all, you can only tell so many lies before they catch up with you."

◉

Berl Bernhard, owner of the struggling Washington Federals (USFL), after another loss: "I feel like Job. I'd rather be the phoenix rising from the ashes, but the ashes keep piling up."

◉

University of Maryland coach Mark Duffner, about North Carolina's two fine tailbacks, Curtis Johnson and Leon Johnson: "I used to think about Johnson and Johnson as a remedy. With these guys, it's an infection for us."

◉

Neale Smith, prep coach and businessman in Maryland, on how big you must be to play football: "If you're good enough, you're big enough."

◉

Red Blaik, longtime Army coach: "Good fellows are a dime a dozen, but an aggressive leader is priceless."

◉

Paul Brown, upon facing the Kansas City Awesome Foursome that averaged 6'7": "If they stand up, we'll have to throw dirigibles."

🏈

Bum Phillips: "There are two kinds of coaches. Them that's been fired and them that will be fired."

🏈

Dick Vermeil, former coach of the Philadelphia Eagles: "Football has affected my family's entire life style. My little boy won't go to bed unless we give him a two-minute warning."

🏈

Canisius College football coach Tom Hersey, on freshman running back Mike Panepinto, who is 5 foot 4: "He's the only running back I know who has to leave the ground to get a hand-off."

🏈

Temple football coach Ron Dickerson, after his team had been out-scored 186-14 in the first three games: "We're not rebuilding; this is giving birth."

🏈

Dick Crum, University of North Carolina coach, upset over the actions of some Maryland fans, replied when asked if there was anything the conference might propose to control fan behavior: "They might consider barbed wire and land mines."

🏈

Pete Carlesimo, football coach and raconteur: "I think Buff Donelli is one of the greatest coaches in the country. I'm not saying that because he's Italian—but because I am."

🏈

Hank Stram, about his wife, Phyllis: "We met at Purdue. She was a drum majorette, sang with a band, had her own radio show, gave baton lessons, and was a brilliant student. She was definitely a No. 1 draft choice."

🏈

Philadelphia Eagles' Marion Campbell, on the three quarterbacks (Ron Jaworski, Joe Pisarcik, and Dan Pastorini) he tried during a 23-0 loss to the N.Y. Giants: "Hell, if we'd have had Mandrake in there Sunday, it wouldn't have made any difference."

Bud Grant, Minnesota Vikings' coach, on man-on-man pass coverage: "The only good thing about man-on-man coverage is you know who to blame."

Tom Landry, Cowboys' coach, on the progress of a rookie tackle: "The boy is progressing fast. He's already holding like a veteran."

Chuck Shelton, on how great it felt to be carried off the field after Drake's six early-season victories in 1981: "When I die, I want to be embalmed in a sitting position and carried to my grave by two football players."

John McKay, when asked about his team's execution after a horrendous loss to the Bears: "I'm all for it."

Bum Phillips, on how he wants a player to feel after losing: "I want every bone in his head to hurt."

Sam Rutigliano, on whether the Browns had prepared anything special against Seattle's left-handed thrower, Jim Zorn: "We're not worried. All of our defensive backs are right-handed hitters."

Darrell Royal, after watching Earl Campbell being smothered by the Steelers: "All great backs look the same when there's no place to go."

Monte Clark, Detroit Lions, on Larry Csonka: "When he goes on safari, the lions roll up their windows."

Woody Widenhofer, Vanderbilt coach, on what he wanted his team to show against Alabama: "The kind of confidence that the 82-year-old man had when he married a 25-year-old woman and bought a five room house next to an elementary school."

Don James, University of Washington football coach on the advantages of having a player on the Playboy pre-season all-star team: "I like it because it's the one month out of the year my wife lets me buy the magazine."

🏈

Vince Lombardi: "Some people try to find things in this game that don't exist. Football is two things. It's blocking and tackling."

🏈

Weeb Ewbank, former Jet , asked to assess Joe Namath's performance in a stage production of Picnic: "I'll have to wait until I see the films."

🏈

Frustrated football coach about his team's inconsistent play: "One week we play like King Kong, the next week like Fay Wray."

🏈

Bobby Ross, University of Maryland football coach, lamenting the youthfulness of his 1984 squad: "We're so young that we might start burping our players at night."

🏈

Paul "Bear" Bryant, on the importance of football: "We're supposed to be living in a very sophisticated time, with sophisticated young people, all worldly-wise and knowledgeable. How can the game of football still be important in that context? I'll tell you how I feel. I feel it's more important than ever. What else have we got to anchor to? Where else can we walk out there even—same everything—and compete? Look around. Maybe the football field's the only place left. Maybe we've already lost it everywhere else."

🏈

Amos Alonzo Stagg, on his 100th birthday: "I may go on forever because statistics show that few men die after the age of 100."

🏈

Jack Molesworth, Western Maryland College coach, on winning: "Winning isn't everything, but losing isn't anything."

🏈

Sam Rutigliano of the Cleveland Browns, on Raider boss Al Davis: "Al is the kind of guy who would steal your eyes and try to convince you that you look better without them."

Tom Flores, Raiders' coach, about image: "If the Redskins are a family, then we're an orphanage."

University of Miami coach Dennis Erickson, describing a football fan: "A typical fan is a guy who sits on the 40, criticizes the coaches and the players and has all the answers. Then he leaves the stadium and can't find his car."

Joe Kapp's scouting report on his prize defensive recruit, Joel Dickson: "He's 6-5, 245, eats garlic and likes to hang around quarterbacks."

Mike Rentko, Associate Head Coach, St. Paul's School (Brooklandville, Md.), after scouting a key rival: "If their linemen were any bigger, they'd have their own zip code."

Two dispirited coaches, who just lost tough games: *Mike:* "Hey Ike, what do you call two football referees working in a shoe store?" *Ike:* "Mike, that's easy—a pair of loafers!"

Sam Rutigliano, Cleveland Browns' coach, on why he doesn't wear a head set on the sidelines: "It doesn't go with the type of hair spray I use."

Steve Owen, former coach, New York Giants: "Football is a game that can't be played with diagrams on a blackboard; you have to get down on the ground with the other fellow and find out who's the better man."

Chuck Mills, Wake Forest coach, on half-time speeches: "I give the same half-time speech over and over. It works best when my players are better than the other coach's players."

Bum Phillips, New Orleans' coach, about Don Shula: "He can take his'n and beat your'n, or take your'n and beat his'n."

Chapter 12

Lee Corso, explaining why Southern Cal was put on the Indiana schedule (while he was coaching there): "When I took this job, I promised our fans I'd show them a Rose Bowl team."

Abe Lemons, while University of Texas basketball coach: "I'd rather be a football coach. That way you can only lose eleven games."

Bowden Wyatt, Tenessee football coach, on pursuit: "Pursuit means getting to the ball with the least possible delay—and in bad humor!"

George Allen on winning: "Winning is living. Every time you win, you're reborn. When you lose, you die a little."

Coach Bum Phillips about star running back, Earl Campbell: "He might not be in a class by himself, but it doesn't take long to call the roll."

Mark Reuss, Assistant at St. Paul's School, (Brooklandville, Md.), to his Head Coach after he had scouted a formidable opponent: "Their lineman are so big, it only takes three to make a dozen."

Bill Parcells, N.Y. Giants' coach, after putting Butch Woolfolk back into a lopsided game so that Woolfolk could carry the ball three more times and set an NFL single game record of 45 carries, and then being asked, "What would you have done if he had been injured?" "Just what any other coach would have done—killed myself."

Vince Lombardi on football: "A school without football is in danger of deteriorating into a medieval study hall."

Baltimore Colts coach, Frank Kush, asked about a late T.D. scored by an opponent: "Well, we were in a nickel defense, but played it like a penny."

Los Angeles Raiders' coach Tom Flores, on his 1984 pre-season quarterback situation: "Jim (Plunkett) is No. 1 and Marc (Wilson) No. $1^{1/2}$.

Steve Owen, former New York Giants' coach, describing Bronko Nagurski: "He was the only man I ever saw who ran his own interference."

Pessimistic coach bemoaning his woes: "I don't mean to put down our QB, but playing him is like going to war with kitchen utensils."

Charlie Havens, successful and respected Western Maryland College mentor, to former player who as a young college coach was attending his first meeting of the American Football Coaches Association: "Let me give you some good advice. You're going to be nervous here at first. You'll be dazzled by all the great coaches you're going to meet. But don't take it too seriously. The first day you're here, you'll wonder how you made it. After that, you'll wonder how the rest of us made it."

Marv Levy, Buffalo Bills' coach, when asked prior to one of his Super Bowl defeats if the game was a "must-win": "No, World War II was a 'must-win.'"

Hayden Fry, Iowa football coach, on first things: "The first thing I said when I came on this campus is that before you can start winning you have to stop losing."

Tom Flores, L. A. Raiders' coach on pre-game prayer: "When you say a prayer and then go out and try to rip some guy's head off, it's kind of a contradiction to what you just did. I guess that's why on our team it's a silent prayer."

John McKay, Tampa Bay football coach, in his post-game remarks after his club took a clobbering from the underdog New Orleans Saints, 42-14: "After you shower, if anybody thinks he really needs a shower ..."

Coach Doug Duvall of Wilde Lake High School (Md.) complimenting an opponent after a close game: "We were throwing the kitchen sink at them, but they were pulling the plug and just draining it."

Duffy Daugherty, Michigan State's legendary coach, describing a less than financially successful visit to the Santa Anita racetrack: "This is the only place I know where windows clean people."

Steve Sloan, Ole Miss coach, on one of the problems of being away on the banquet circuit too long: "My wife fixed fried chicken for dinner, and the next thing I knew I was standing at the table, welcoming my family, asking for their support, and giving a quick run-down on the Ole Miss team."

Boston College coach Jack Bicknell on B.C.'s 5-foot-9 quarterback Doug Flutie and whether pro scouts believe he is too small: "The pro scouting computer will blow up when they put his name in it."

Dick Harlow, the late, great coach who led teams at Western Maryland College and Harvard, on responding to critics: "I have made it a rule not to get into squirting contests with skunks."

John McKay, Tampa Bay coach, on the future of Bill Capece, who had a disappointing season as the team's placekicker: "Capece is kaput."

Mike Rentko, Associate Head Coach, St. Paul's School (Brooklandville, Md.), evaluating Lincoln Bogart, an especially skilled player who ran, passed, punted, kicked extra points, kicked off, played safety on defense, and ran back punts and kick-offs: "Boy, he's put more guys out of work than Cyrus McCormick's reaper."

Phil Jackman, Baltimore Evening Sun columnist, on football players: "In the immortal words of Knute Rockne, 'The only qualifications for a lineman are to be big and dumb. To be a back, you only have to be dumb.'"

Joe Paterno, Penn State's highly-respected coach after turning down a $1.3 million offer to become coach of the Boston Patriots: "Nobody in football is worth a million dollars. It's ridiculous."

George Allen, former NFL coach, on losing: "Losing is worse than death because you have to get up the next morning."

Monte Clark, Detroit Lions' coach, on his hometown of Kingsburg, California: "It's so small that the number one industry is taking bottles back to the store."

Oklahoma coach Barry Switzer on why Nebraska's Mike Rozier is the best back ever to play in the Big 8: "He makes all his linemen think they're All-Americans with the way he goes about his business."

Sam Rutigliano, Cleveland Browns' coach, on how to stop Seattle's scrambling quarterback, Jim Zorn: "Well, you could give your outside linebackers hand grenades."

Coach Ron Meyer of New England on why Mosi Tatupu has so much success in bad weather since he was born in American Samoa, raised in Hawaii and played at U.S.C.: "Mosi is just a great surfer."

Darrell Royal, former head football coach at Texas, on being head coach: "A head coach is guided by one primary objective: to dig, claw, wheedle, coax that fanatical effort out of his players to play on Saturdays as if they were planting the flag on Iwo Jima."

Barry Switzer on Marcus Dupree: "Marcus Dupree came here [to Oklahoma] with E.T. He's from a different world."

🏈

Duffy Daugherty, summarizing his passing philosophy: "Only three things can happen when you put the ball up in the air, and two of them are bad."

🏈

Dick Harlow, after his brawny Harvard team was beaten by a smaller but brainier opponent, responding to a friend who said, "Don't feel bad. Remember that a brainy team always would beat a team that was merely brawn." "Yeah, I'll crawl into a ring with Einstein any day."

🏈

Tom Mueller, Texas Christian University defensive coordinator, explaining to exasperated Head Coach Jim Wacker why there was no Horned Frog defender near an opposing receiver who had just dropped a pass in the end zone: "Coach, if they're not going to catch them, we're not going to cover them."

🏈

Rick Forzano, former Navy coach, recalling a trouncing by Michigan: "You know how their band plays 'Hail to the Victors' after each touchdown? Well, by the second quarter, I found myself humming the tune. By the third quarter, I knew all the words. By the fourth quarter, I was singing along with them. It's a catchy song."

🏈

Iowa Eddie Anderson, after his team edged Purdue by the unusual score of 4-0: "We had it clinched with the first safety, but we wanted to run up the score."

🏈

Ron Meyer, while coach at S.M.U., on his 5-9, 220-lb. guard: "McAtee is so short his breath smells of earthworms."

🏈

Rick Collins, Associate Head Coach at St. Paul's School (Brooklandville, Md.): "When someone tells you that nothing is impossible—ask him to dribble a football."

🏈

Vince Lombardi, on winning: "Winning isn't everything—but wanting to win is."

Barry Switzer, Oklahoma coach, after making a neat catch of an out-of-bounds pass by the Nebraska quarterback: "Would they have penalized me if I had spiked the ball?"

Bud Grant, Minnesota Vikings' mentor, on coaches who work 18 hours a day: "I don't think time represents work."

Barry Switzer, on Oklahoma's great back, Mike Rozier: "He plays mad every down."

Legendary Alabama football coach, Bear Bryant, in Gainesville, FL, for an Alabama–Florida game years ago, called room service for breakfast. "I'd like two raw sausage patties, burned toast, some blackened scrambled eggs and lukewarm coffee," he said. The hotel waiter protested: "Sir, we can't send you an order like that."

Bryant: "The hell you can't. That's what I got yesterday."

Lou Holtz, on advice: "My athletes are always willing to accept my advice, as long as it doesn't conflict with their view."

Chapter 13

Arizona State Bruce Snyder after viewing film of his team's upset of Washington, 32-17: "It was like the stew my mom used to make. It was even better the second day."

❧

J.T. King, Texas Tech coach, showing his dread of an intercepted pass, sending a play in the game with his end: "Tell the quarterback to throw it to you if you're open, and to me if you're not."

❧

Eddie Robinson, great Grambling coach, on winning: "Gotta have the horses to make the wagon go."

❧

John McKay, Buccaneers' coach, on his running feud with the fans in 1983: "My humor was appreciated in California [when he coached at Southern California] but it goes over the heads of people in Florida."

❧

Sam Rutigliano, when asked if linebacker Tom Coustineau was good enough to warrant a salary of $500,000 a year: "Nobody'll ever play that good."

❧

Coach Archie Cooley of Mississippi Valley State extolling the virtues of his ace receiver, Jerry Rice, who caught 24 passes in one game: "He could catch a BB in the dark."

❧

Pepper Rodgers, relating what he told his wife after a terrible season at U.C.L.A. when he was taking a lot of heat: "My dog was about my only friend, and I told my wife that a man needs at least two friends. She agreed—and bought me another dog."

❧

Tad Jones, legendary coach of Yale University, reminding his 1923 team before the Harvard game: "Gentlemen, you are about to play Harvard. You will never do anything else so important the rest of your lives."

🏈

Allie Sherman, former N.Y. Giants' coach, on his confrontation with an unwelcome visitor to his practice:

Sherman: "You have to leave, this is a secret practice."

Visitor: "What have you got to hide?"

🏈

Chuck O'Connell, Washington and Lee defensive coordinator, accolading a watch-charm guard: "Oh, he's big! He's just not tall."

🏈

Mike Gottfried, Kansas coach, when asked if his review of Nebraska game films had provided him with any clue as to what it is the Cornhuskers do that other college football teams don't: "I've never seen anyone kick off so much."

🏈

Disgruntled Coach, who had just lost badly to a cross-town rival, asked how many men he had on his team:

"About half."

🏈

Bum Phillips, New Orleans' coach on building a team: "There are two ways to build a team. You either get better players or get the players you've got to play better."

🏈

Joe Salem, Minnesota coach, before the 1-6 Gophers lost by a score of 19-8 Saturday to 1-6 Northwestern: "This is the battle of the movable defense versus the stoppable force."

🏈

Coach Charlie Winner, exasperated after watching quarterback Jim Hart throw eight straight incompleted passes: "Jim, if it wasn't for the law of gravity, you wouldn't even hit the ground."

🏈

Jim Hanifan, St. Louis Cardinal coach, inviting reporters to serve as tackling dummies for the football team, which lost its first three games: "It could give you some extra pay, and you've got a good chance of not getting hit."

❦

Bill Yeoman, University of Houston coach, bemoaning the fact that 300-pound senior tackle Earl Jones had been declared ineligible: "He can move around pretty good. He just didn't move to class too well."

❦

Sam Bailey, while a coach at Tampa University, expressing mixed feelings about a big interior lineman he was recruiting: "He's big as a gorilla and strong as a gorilla. Now if he were as smart as a gorilla, he'd be fine."

❦

L.A. Rams running back coach, on Eric Dickerson: "When he runs by you, you don't even hear him. Usually with a big back, you hear a clump. With him, there's just a 'Whoosh.'"

❦

Bill Parcells on former coach Sam Wyche predicting the N.Y. Jets would win the AFC West: "I think Sam ought to lie on a coach and talk to somebody quietly, maybe with a little Montavani playing in the background."

❦

Joe Paterno, wondering about Richard Nixon: "How could President Nixon have known as much about college football in 1969 and so little about Watergate in 1972?"

❦

Ron Meyer, while coaching at SMU, on Rice's 6'8" tight end, Robert Hubble: "When he's covered, he's open."

❦

Cal Stoll, Minnesota coach on Nebraska: "This year we've got Nebraska right where we want them—off the schedule."

❦

Joe Paterno, on coaches:"All coaches are thinking men or else they wouldn't survive."

Chicago Bears's assistant coach, on a draft choice who was highly regarded because of his versatility: "He is a versatile guy. So far we've found six positions he can't play."

Bum Phillips, after his South team lost to the North in the Senior Bowl game: "Now I know why the South lost the Civil War. They must have had the same officials."

Sam Rutigliano, Cleveland Browns' coach, explaining a loss: "If you can't make the putts and can't get the man in from second in the bottom of the ninth, you're not going to win enough football games in this league, and that's the problem we had today."

Ron Meyer, New England Patriots' coach, on democracy and football: "We run a very autocratic democracy here. That means I say what goes but I listen to you."

Nebraska football coach Tom Osborne, on how he has been since the Cornhuskers lost the 1984 Orange Bowl game to Miami (31-30): "I sleep like a baby. I sleep for an hour, then I wake up and cry for an hour."

Gunther Cunningham, Baltimore Colts' defensive line coach: "The criteria for defensive linemen is sacks, tackles, and quarterback pressures. And it's how many have you got for me lately."

Bill Walsh, San Francisco 49-ers' coach, after benching running back Wendell Tyler following his second fumble vs. Chicago: "I decided for his sake and for ours to get him out of there."

Tom Landry, Dallas coach, on whether he and quarterback Roger Staubach discussed, during a time-out, whether to go for the first down, or attempt a field goal: "We discussed it, but there was no vote."

John Mackovic, Kansas City Chiefs' coach, on being prepared: "You must always be prepared for today. If you lose sight of that, then you will never have a today, which was a tomorrow yesterday. What I'm saying is, you must be prepared for today, because tomorrow really doesn't ever get here from yesterday, and we have to assume it will get here again tomorrow."

Larry Lacewell, assistant coach at Oklahoma, on the Sooners tough schedule: "I can't figure how we missed scheduling Russia."

Chuck Knox, Seattle Seahawks' coach: "Football is not an ad-lib game."

Coach Don Nehlen of West Virginia, on Maryland's quarterback Boomer Esiason: "The only way to stop Esiason, even when he isn't physically sound, is to drop down on your knees and pray."

Howard Schnellenberger, University of Miami coach, asked whether he'd consider jumping to the USFL if he were offered a million-a-year deal: "You mean you want me to take a pay cut just because we lost to Florida?"

Nick Coso, after being fired after Ferris State went 0-8 in 1983: "It was a building year, but the building caved in on me."

Howard Schnellenberger, on why he caught so many passes in crowds as a high school end: "I was too slow to get out of any crowd."

Shug Jordan, Auburn's great coach, on why he gave up pitching baseball and turned to football: "One day I threw my fastball and hit a guy right between the eyes. It didn't even faze him. He just tossed his bat away and trotted down to first. I decided right then and there that it was time to quit."

Chapter 14

Tampa Bay Bucs' coach John McKay, on why he'll return in 1984 despite a 2-14 season: "I'm not burned out. Sometimes I'm burned up, but not out."

Cleveland Browns' coach, Sam Rutigliano on the future of the USFL: "If God had meant for us to play football in the spring, he wouldn't have invented baseball."

Joe Paterno, Penn State coach, upon being questioned after three straight losses: "We've started a new quiz game. We call it 'Where's my line.'"

Bud Grant, on humor: "Somebody without humor is the most boring person in the world. If you can't appeal to somebody's humor once in awhile, life gets to be an awful bore."

George Mitchell, three-sport star at Johns Hopkins University, and a successful coach in Maryland, on fortitude: "It's not the size of the dog in the fight, it's the size of the fight in the dog."

Ed Januszkiewicz, Recreation League Coach and football adherent: "If at first you don't succeed, you're doing about average."

Woody Hayes, former Ohio State coach, on sports: "Anyone who will tear down sports in America will tear down America. Sports and religion have made America what it is today."

Mike White, University of Illinois coach, whose team lost to UCLA, 45-9, in the 1984 Rose Bowl, on the highlight: "The only highlight for me was when the scoreboard went out."

🏈

Coach Donnie Duncan, whose Iowa State team had just been clobbered by Nebraska, on how good the Cornhuskers were: "There are lots of teams better than Nebraska. Fortunately, most of them are in the NFL."

🏈

Bob Zuppke, successful Illinois coach of yesteryear: "All quitters are good losers."

🏈

Bob Zuppke of Illinois, frankly hesitant about scheduling Knute Rockne's tough Notre Dame Club, discussing the situation with Rockne:

Rockne: "But I'm losing my first team through graduation."
Zuppke: "No, can't do it."
Rockne: "I'm also losing my second team through graduation."
Zuppke: "Sorry Rock, but I don't think your third team would draw in Champaign."

🏈

Don Matthews, coach of the Canadian Football League's B.C. Lions asked whether his team would try any quick kicks in an upcoming game in Vancouver's domed stadium: "Only when we have the air conditioning at our backs."

🏈

Bengal Sam Wyche, addressing linebacker Rick Hunley's continuing holdout: "You wish there could have been a nice harmonious marriage. But right now as far as I'm concerned, the courtship is over. We've already sent all the candy and flowers we're going to send."

🏈

Paul Brown, frustrated after yelling at the officials, but to no avail, when one of his tackles is held so obviously, he has two pieces of his jersey ripped off by the defensive end: "All right so that end didn't rip out those holes in the jersey. It must have been moths."

🏈

Coach John Mackovic of Wake Forest, when asked if his team's 22-21 upset victory over Georgia was the biggest win of his coaching career: "Well, it certainly ranks up there with the top three. Why? I have only three wins so far."

🏈

Sam Rutigliano, Cleveland Browns' coach, on Defensive End, Carl Hairston: "Yes, Carl has a gut and a big butt, but that's where his power comes from. Carl is living proof that you don't have to have a body that looks like it was etched from a Greek statue. I've seen a lot of guys like that working on the turnpike.?

🏈

Ron Erhardt, New England Patriot coach, on why his receivers, coached by Raymond Berry, now assistant coach, were dropping so many passes: "Simple. Raymond is coachin' em, not catchin' em."

🏈

Coaches of America, hopefully optimistic:
A coach knocked at the Pearly Gates.
His face was scarred and cold;
He stood before the man of fate
For Admission to the Fold
What have you done, St. Peter asked,
To gain admission here?
I've been a Coach, sir, he said,
For many and many a year.
The Pearly Gates swung open wide,
St. Peter touched the bell.
Come in, he said, and choose your harp,
You've had your share of hell.

🏈

Duffy Daugherty, Michigan State mentor, after his team had stopped both Notre Dame and Indiana inches short of touchdowns: "I like these goal line stands of ours but I wish they would make them around the 50 yard line. I could see them better."

🏈

Bobby Bowden, Florida State football coa[ch] one of his star defensemen: "He doesn't know the meaning of th[e] [wo]rd 'fear.' In fact, I just saw his grades and he doesn't know the [mean]ing of a lot of words."

🏈

Ivy League football coach who had just completed a [roug]h season, on why a rowing race held some fascination for him: "It's th[e o]nly sport I know where you could sit on your butt and win going back[wa]rd."

🏈

Joe Gibbs, Washington Redskins' coach, declining credit f[or] the one back offense popularized by his team: "I wasn't even in the r[oo]m when it was invented."

🏈

Dallas Cowboy Tom Landry, on golfer Byron Nelson's amazing accuracy: "He couldn't play 36 holes in one day over the same course because the second time around, he'd be hitting out of the same divot."

🏈

A Green Bay assistant coach commenting on Fran Tarkenton's early years with Minnesota: "All you had to do was wave your arm and you'd scare him out of the pocket. But you still needed a butterfly net to catch him."

🏈

Ray Perkins, Alabama football coach, after Ken Stabler, an NFL free agent, failed to appear at a recent banquet: "He's probably been traded to another banquet."

🏈

Doug Duvall, highly successful coach at Wilde Lake High School (MD), about the program he inherited—it was 2-7 and was the Homecoming game for seven opponents: "We were so many people's Homecoming game that I thought we should have had our own float."

🏈

Pittsburgh coach Chuck Noll on the departure of Franco Harris from the Pittsburgh Steelers: "It's a tragedy. If you're Shakespearean, you'd enjoy it."

🏈

Bill Parcel Y. Giants' coach, on why the Giants couldn't melt down their 3. defensive end, Leonard Marshall: "We put him on the Cambric et and he ate half of Harvard."

●

Joe G , on the motivational power of his weight-lifting coach, Dan Rile I once looked up at the ceiling and saw a spider doing a bench p ss."

●

ry Switzer, Oklahoma coach describing defensive nose guard Top Casillas: "He's got feet like a sewing machine."

●

Bobby Bowden, on his initial reaction when approached about the possibility of taking the head coaching job at Florida State University which had one of the losingest college football programs in the country: "I could think of only two jobs that could have been worse:
1) Being elected mayor of Atlanta shortly after Sherman left town.
2) Being the general who volunteers to replace George Custer during the last siege at Little Big Horn."

●

Mike Gottfried, Kansas football coach, on learning that the odds against his Jayhawks winning the Big Eight title are 100 to 1: "Who's the one guy who thinks we can do it."

●

Cleveland Browns' Sam Rutigliano, on learning that wide receiver Dwight Walker had not been seriously hurt in a wee-small-hours auto accident: "I'm going to ask him what the hell he was doing out at 3:37 in the morning. If things aren't kosher, I'll fine him up to a week's pay for conduct detrimental to the Browns. I can't make a player say 10 Hail Marys and 10 Our Fathers and promise he won't do it again."

●

Chapter 15

Terry Brennan, former Notre Dame , on losing: "If you're old and you lose, they say you're outmoded. If you're young and you lose, they say you're green. So don't lose."

Phil Albert, Towson University (Md.) coach, after one of his captains, a defensive stalwart, was expelled from school: "Our players are concerned with his absence. But I have told them that in our football program we are like Cadillacs. When someone buys a Cadillac he demands performance. We're not Mavericks. You don't expect much from a Maverick."

Buddy Ryan, Philadelphia Eagles' coach, on his relationship with his former boss, Mike Ditka of the Bears: "Ditka and I never had a confrontation. I'd put the game plan on his secretary's desk when I finished it, and she would put it on his desk. Not that he'd understand much of it ..."

Dick Vermeil, former Eagles' coach and CBS analyst, about Bill Bain, the L. A. Rams' large offensive tackle: "He's so big they don't get him a locker, they get him a corral."

John Robinson, L. A. Rams' coach, on whether QB Dieter Brock might have lost confidence after his poor 6-22 game against the Cowboys: "No, but if he has a bad game on Sunday, I think it will have an effect on his confidence, because he won't be playing anymore this season."

Chuck Mooney, on the persuasive powers of T.C.U. coach Jim Wacker: "He could sell screen doors to a submarine commander."

Art Guepe, Virginia football coach from 1945 to 1952, surveying his fat old players at a homecoming reunion: "At last, you're big enough to play football."

Chuck Knox, Seattle Seahawks' coach, defending his predilection toward uttering adages, mottos, and inspirational sayings: "Most of my cliches aren't original."

Monte Clark, deposed Detroit Lions' coach, tired of criticism from players after QB Eric Hipple said he lost confidence under Clark: "I think that feeling was well-founded. He threw a lot of great 50-yard passes. Unfortunately, the receivers were 45 yards away."

Ted Marchibroda, the Buffalo Bills' offensive coordinator and former Head Coach of the Baltimore Colts: "I'd rather be an assistant and win than be a head coach and lose."

Cumberland University (Lebanon, Tn.) football coach, Nick Coutras, recounting some difficulties encountered in starting football there: "We had 82 fellows show up for our first practice. They all didn't stay around. Some walk-ons found that when the fur starts flying and some of it's theirs, it's not as much fun as it looks on TV."

Bill Parcells, Giant coach, about tight end Mark Bavarro's surgery on his knee and whether he would be ready for the season opener: "It won't get that far. It will go to a certain point, and we'll assume he either will be there or won't be there."

Hank Stram about the upcoming season: "It's going to be a stock-market season—up and down for all teams."

George E. Allen on losers: "Rockne wanted nothing but 'bad losers.' Good losers get into the habit of losing."

Walt Michaels, veteran coach of several pro teams, on fear: "A man who has no fear belongs in a mental institution or on special teams."

●

N.Y. Giants' coach Bill Parcells on why he calls cornerback Elvis Patterson "Toast": "Because he gets burned so much."

●

Coach Bill Walsh of San Francisco, responding to fellow coach John Robinson's comment that the 49-ers were capable of winning nine straight: "John is one of the most gracious men I've ever known. He gave Argentina a lot of hope in the Falkland Islands."

●

Tony Demeo, Mercyhurst coach, after a game played on a sloppy field: "It was so muddy, people planted rice at halftime."

●

Vanderbilt coach Watson Brown discussing the progress of his team: "There's a light at the end of the tunnel. I just hope it's not a gorilla with a flashlight."

●

Mike Ditka, on Refrigerator Perry's claim that he is a light eater: "He's absolutely right. As soon as it's light, he starts eating."

●

Coach Bill Parcells of the Giants on his upcoming game with the L. A. Rams: "We're going to have to do things a little differently. I really don't have to get hit in the face with a skunk three times before I smell it."

●

Houston Oilers' Jerry Glanville, on 266-pound guard Mike Kelly: "He was threatening to retire this year but said he was afraid to go home because he was afraid his dad would kick his butt. I told him, 'If you do go home, send me your dad.'"

●

Clemson defensive coordinator Tom Harper, who coached William "The Refrigerator" Perry and also his 270-pound younger brother, Michael Dean: "I'm kinda the Will Rogers of Clemson. I've never met a Perry I didn't like."

Chicago Bears' Mike Ditka on the Green Bay Packers verbal line-backer, Tim Harris: "Sometimes, God gives you great physical talent and takes away the brain."

Howard University coach Willie Jeffries, whose line averaged over 300 pounds, about their culinary habits: "In restaurants, we don't ask for a menu, we get an estimate."

Sam Rutigliano, former coach of the Cleveland Browns who is now coaching at a Liberty University in Lynchburg, Va., about the pressure of coaching: "As long as they've got a scoreboard, there'll be pressure."

Spike Dykes, of the Texas Tech Red Raiders after they beat Texas (24-17) for the first time in 22 years at Austin: "You keep scratchin' and sooner or later you dig up worms."

Philadelphia Eagles' Buddy Ryan on his relationship with owner Norman Braman: "We're good friends now. I think he knows I'm doing a hell of a job. I've told him enough times."

Indianapolis Colts' Ron Meyer on the pressure of working for owner Bob Irsay: "My owner doesn't want green bananas. He wants results now."

Nebraska football coach Tom Osborne, recalling his two-year stint as an end for the Redskins: "We had an incentive pay system. You got money for such things as yards, completions, fumble recoveries. When we added it all together, I owed the team $34.50."

When the Giants played the Cardinals, the game featured New York's 31 year old running back Ottis Anderson while Phoenix countered with 30 year old Stump Mitchell, prompting Giants' Bill Parcells to quip: "They don't ask for your birth certificate when you get in the huddle."

🏈

Coach Mack Brown, after Tulane lost it's first seven games: "I called up Dial-A-Prayer and they hung up on me."

🏈

Bobby Bowden, after watching Miami of Florida blast his top-ranked Florida State Seminoles, 31-0, in what had been billed as the "College Game of the Century": "It was a Classic until we kicked it off."

🏈

Ray Sewault, T.C.U. recruiting coordinator, about his team: "We've got so many kids on our roster (70 sophs and frosh) we're going to be the first football team in history with an equipment order for Pampers."

🏈

Doug Weaver, former Kansas State University coach, on being hanged in effigy: "I'm glad it happened in front of the library. I've always emphasized scholarship."

🏈

John Bridgers, upon taking over Baylor's football program: "We're going to be optimistic like the three good Baptists who were ship-wrecked on a desert island and immediately arranged a Sunday School attendance goal of four."

🏈

Arizona State offensive tackle coach Tom Freeman, on a cardinal sin: "It's better to die at birth than jump off-sides at the goal line."

🏈

Buddy Ryan, Eagles' coach, to Mike Quick, who after he was elected captain asked if that meant he would have the authority to exert more power and make decisions: "Yeah. You can call 'Heads or tails' on the coin toss."

🏈

Tubby Raymond, University of Delaware coach, on the fact that his team doesn't have a booster club: "Why should I organize my own lynch mob."

🏈

Darrell Royal, former University of Texas coach: "I see only one big difference in players today. They write more books."

Chapter 16

Bobby Bowden, Florida State coach on faith: "You want to know what a real test of faith is? That's when you go to church and reach into your pocket and all you've got is a $20 bill."

Barry Wilburn's scouting report on receiver Roy Green: "He has two speeds—here he comes and there he goes."

Houston coach Jerry Glanville after a Halloween 'Jerry Glanville look-alike contest': "I told the winner he looked just like me and I'll apologize to his parents."

Ridge Warfield, Boys' Latin School (Baltimore, MD) coach, on why he didn't ever predict how his team would do: "He who lives by the crystal ball ends up eating ground glass."

Sam Goodwin, coach at Northeast Louisiana, after telling his players to use chewing gum to keep their ears from popping on air flights: "It worked fine, except some guys had a hard time getting the gum out of their ears."

Weeb Ewbank, former pro coach, on why rollout passing is like drunken driving: "Speed down the highway long enough and you're sure to get killed."

Former Oilers' coach Bill Peterson, noted for his Yogi Berraisms: "Don't you guys think for a minute that I'm going to take this loss standing down."

Darrell Royal, former Texas football coach on why he wouldn't want the job these days: "We bent the rules, but not like now. I was watching the game between Florida State and Miami. They should have started it with a burglar alarm."

East Carolina Coach Bill Lewis on films: "Watching the Miami-Florida State game on film is like watching an R-rated movie because of violence. We had to check the ages of our players to see if they can watch R movies."

Seattle Seahawks' coach Chuck Knox on his football career: "There's two things in coaching. One is winning and two is misery."

Coach Bill Parcells of the Giants, after watching a major league baseball game attended by 850 fans: "The place was so empty they could have had javelin practice."

Buddy Parker, reviewing an old Chicago Bear film: "Their defensive line play was so dirty it left a ring around the screen."

Lou Holtz, the well-traveled, much respected and highly successful football mentor, is also a purveyor of spiffy bons mots. About the stamp made up in his honor when he was at Arkansas, he said: "After I lost two games, they stopped making it because people began spitting on the wrong side."

Lee Corso, asked what he has been doing since being fired as Indiana football coach: "I've cleaned my basement 14 times. I have the cleanest basement in America."

Chuck Knox, coach of the Seattle Seahawks on the "breaks": "They say the breaks all even up in the long run, but how many of us last that long."

Dick Jauron, Chicago Bears' coach, after winning in his debut: "My favorite offensive formation is taking a knee. I love that formation."

Larry Bruno, Joe Namath's football coach at Beaver Falls High School, commenting on the fact that Namath called about 99 percent of the team's plays: "I let him. I wasn't about to screw things up."

Bum Phillips, former Houston coach, after he passed his physical: "Well, at least if I drop dead tomorrow, I'll know I died in good health."

Dan Reeves, on whether it's an advantage to play the Raiders after a Monday night game: "Absolutely—if you can play them on Tuesday night."

Lou Holtz, on the speed of one of his Notre Dame teams: "We don't have much sped. We can't run sweeps for fear of a delay of game penalty."

Jerry Glanville, coach of the Atlanta Falcons, when he heard that Dallas Cowboy coach Jimmy Johnson claims to work 18 hours a day: "That's impossible. It takes 12 to comb his hair."

Coach Bill Parcells of the Giants, pointing out two positives in their loss at Anaheim: "It was sunny and we looked good warming up."

Sam Wyche, Cincinnati Bengals' coach, on what happened when he ran out on the field to stop a brawl and found himself being pulled one way by one official and another way by a second official: "I heard one of them say, 'Make a Wyche.'"

LaVell Edwards, BYU football coach, on why he likes Sherlock Holmes: "I just love those guys who win 'em all."

Ray Perkins, Tampa Bay coach, on the importance of linemen: "The people who win games for you are those who put their hands on the ground."

🏈

Bobby Bowden, Florida State's philosophic coach, when they were touted as the No. 1 team: "You know if you drop that halo down just about 12 inches it becomes a noose."

🏈

Coach Bill Parcells, about QB Phil Simms, when he came to camp after his extended holdout: "He's as rusty as a door latch on a Vermont barn."

🏈

Coach Bill Parcells of the Giants, when greeted by 75 reporters at his news conference: "I hope this many people come to my funeral."

🏈

Former Lafayette coach, Edward "Hook" Mylin, after having lost a game by the lopsided score of 46-0, was leaving the stadium and accidentally bumped into a lady on her way out. "Pardon me," he said, "no offense": The lady's response: "You're telling me."

🏈

Kentucky football coach Bill Curry on how tough it was to please writers when he was at Alabama: "There was a joke going around that when I went on a fishing trip, the boat tipped over, but I got to shore by walking on water. The headline in the next day's paper read: 'Curry fails at swimming.'"

🏈

Jeff Cravath, on why he gave up coaching at USC to run a ranch: "Cattle don't have alumni."

🏈

Frustrated coach, upon being informed of unfair criticism by a critical reporter: "He's so dumb he thinks a football coach has four wheels."

🏈

Defensive Coordinator Charlie McBride on No. 8 Nebraska's 7-3 half-time deficit against 51 ? point underdog Oregon State: "We started out like we were playing bridge."

🏈

Liberty University coach Sam Rutigliano, on his team's struggling offense: "It reminded me of the tango. One, two, three, kick."

Arizona football coach Dick Tomey, on using two quarterbacks, a sophomore and a senior: "I think the only time you're not comfortable with two guys is if neither one of them is any good."

Christian Holgard, assistant coach at North Dakota State, who during his entire high school football career, never heard his school's fight song because his team never scored a touchdown: "I was always under the impression that our school song was 'The Star Spangled Banner.'"

Former Iowa State coach George Veenker, to a banquet audience: "I would like to introduce the boy who made our longest run of this season, a run of 90 yards. Unfortunately he didn't catch the man with the ball."

Mike Ditka, coach of the Chicago Bears, asked how he would dress for a Halloween party: "I'd come as a TV reporter. I would have to get some dumb questions ready."

Florida State Bobby Bowden, on his family: "When our first child came, I told my wife, Ann, 'This is our cheerleader.' As our sons came along, I would say, 'This is our quarterback,' or 'This is the center,' and so on. When the sixth child came, Ann said, 'This is the end.'"

Lefty James, Cornell football coach, the first time he saw all-world Jim Brown playing lacrosse: "Oh my goodness, they're letting him play with a stick in his hand!"

Perspicacious Baltimore Ravens fan about second year head coach, Brian Billick: "He may be wrong and he may be opinionated, but he sure as hell is not uncertain."

Chapter 17

Bud Grant, former Minnesota Vikings' coach, on why a dog is a coach's best friend: "He doesn't watch TV. He doesn't know whether you won or lost."

Tulsa coach Don Morton, following his team's 76-14 loss to Florida State: "A loss is a loss. It doesn't matter what the score is. It's like fighting the Russians with very limited bullets."

Colorado football coach Bill McCartney on how to take Notre Dame Lou Holtz's pronouncements: "Whatever he says, I'm sure he means. Except sometimes he changes his mind."

Washington Redskins' defensive coach Richie Petibon, on Philadelphia Eagles' QB Randall Cunningham:
"He's probably the most dangerous player in the game today. It's like playing with a time bomb while walking through a minefield."

Pessimistic coach, describing an upcoming opponent: "Heck, they have first-round picks on their scout squad."

John Ralston, former coach of the Denver Broncos explaining his leaving: "I left because of illness and fatigue. The fans were sick and tired of me."

Mike Ditka, Bears' coach about being clobbered by the Minnesota Vikings: "Once the truck hit me, I did not bother getting up. I just laid there and watched."

Bobby Bowden, Florida State coach during a struggling season: "The good news is that our defense is giving up only one touch-down a game. The bad news is that our offense is doing the same."

Ron Meyer, after his Colts beat the Eagles in a big upset: "It was scary looking over at the Eagle sideline and seeing their backup QB, Jim McMahon, wearing a big Super Bowl ring and then looking at our own QB with his Signa Chi ring from Western Illinois."

Dick MacPherson, 60 years old, upon being named coach of the 1-15 New England Patriots: "It's a young man's game, not matter what your age is. But what the hell is wrong with a 60-year-old man with a young man's enthusiasm? Anybody can be a young coach. The secret is to be an old coach, to hang on."

N. Y. Giants' football coach Bill Parcells on Eagles' coach Buddy Ryan's 30-pound weight loss in an off-season contest: "The other coaches have a new nickname for him now: 'Bud Light.'"

Bo Schembechler, former Michigan coach, on football: "Football is the American game that typifies the old American spirit. It's physical. It's hard work. It's aggressive. You're in battles in which, no matter how you add it up, the entire personality and character of a person is bared. Football is not going to die. It is an American heritage."

Floyd Peters, former defensive coordinator of the Minnesota Vikings, on his feelings about being fired and jobless: "I'm not nervous about it. I was a guard at San Quentin prison in 1955. They paid you $150 a month, room and board, and you got a free shoeshine, haircut, and shave once a week. An inmate holding that razor to your throat giving you that shave – that makes you nervous."

Pepper Rodgers' son, shortly after his dad had been named football coach at U.C.L.A., had been told by his mother not to run around the neighborhood telling everyone he was the son of the new coach. When the minister asked him after church the following Sunday who his daddy was, he responded: "I thought it was Pepper Rodgers, but Mom says it isn't so."

Vince Lombardi on football: "I owe most everything to football, in which I have spent the greater part of my life. And I have never lost my respect, my admiration or my love for what I consider a great game. And each Saturday, after the battle, one group savors victory, another group lives in the bitterness of defeat. The many hurts seem a small price to have paid for having won, and there is no reason at all that is adequate for having lost. To the winner there is one hundred percent fun; and to the loser the only thing left for him is one hundred percent resolution, one hundred percent determination. And it's a game, I think, a great deal like life in that it demands that a man's personal commitment be toward excellence and be toward victory, even though you know that ultimate victory can never be completely won. Yet it must be pursued with all of one's might. And each week there's a new encounter, each year a new challenge. But all of the rings and all of the money and all of the color and all of the display, they linger only in the memory. The spirit, the will to win and the will to excel, these are the things that endure and these are the qualities that are so much more important than any of the events that occasion them. And I'd like to say that the quality of any man's life has got to be a full measure of that man's personal commitment to excellence and to victory, regardless of what field he may be in."

Section III:
The Media

Chapter 18

Phil Wood, versatile and gifted sportscaster in Baltimore-Washington area, about the fact he had been fired several times during the winter: "Every time I've been fired, it's been this time of year and I've finally figured out why. It's because you can't walk a block without seeing piles of logs with signs that say 'fire wood.'"

Jack Buck about the chances of the St. Louis Cardinals: "Probably no better than the Colts. They're going to score some points, but I can't see them stopping anybody ... The offensive line is so good even O. J. Anderson (Cardinals' halfback) can't get through it."

Paul Maguire, NBC analyst, commenting about one of the coaches calling for a measurement to determine if a running play netted a first down: "Boy, if you can't see that isn't a first down you should be in another line of work—like officiating."

Jim Armstrong of the *Denver Post* on a name: "Oklahoma State has a football player named Asoteletanga-amosill Pogi. I'd tell you more about him, but I've already taken up enough of your time."

Steve Tasker, CBS analyst, commenting about the Ravens' Michael McCrory's quick and powerful defensive charges during the Baltmore-San Diego game: "Michael McCrory looks like he's running wind sprints against air."

Pat Hayden, NBC football analyst on one aspect of Nebraska's offense: "Nebraska give the ball to the fullback once every lunar eclipse."

Frank Luber, WCBM radio (Baltimore, MD), relating a story about John Unitas to his morning co-host, Sean Casey: "A friend asked John Unitas how much he might be making if he were playing in the NFL.

Unitas replied: 'Oh, about $500,000.'

His friend: 'Half a million! Why some of these guys are making $2, $3 million and more a year.'

J. Unitas: 'Yeah, but I'm 61 years old.'"

Beano Cook, ESPN analyst, describing Penn State's Joe Paterno: "Joe Paterno always wins in November. The only person who has won more in November is FDR."

Dan Patrick, after a series of bizarre occurrences on the same play—interception, fumble, touchdown—during the Baltimore-Jacksonville game: "The only thing we haven't had on this play is someone on the grassy knoll."

New York *Daily News,* describing the N. Y. Jets stunning loss to the heavy underdog Indianapolis Colts: "The Jets came in reeking of overconfidence. In the end, they just plain reeked."

Pete Axthelm, ESPN analyst, about kickers: "A game settled by kickers is like going to an art gallery and missing the masters to view some finger paintings."

Peter Schmuck, *Baltimore Sun* sportswriter, describing the thrilling Army-Navy game in Baltimore in 2000 which ended up with Navy winning 30-28: "There were seven turnovers, a couple of blocked kicks, and more odd twists and turns than a Florida election."

Play-by-play announcer Brad Nessler, about being the offensive coordinator for Joe Paterno or Steve Spurrier: "It's like being the warm-up comedian for Seinfeld."

Rich Eisen, ESPN *The Magazine,* about former Nebraska coach Tom Osborne winning his Congressional primary race with 71% of the vote: "He would have won with 75%, but he took a knee at the voting booth."

🏈

Doug Brown, *Baltimore Evening Sun* sports writer: "Like a breath of fresh air, there comes every so often a sliver of evidence suggesting that pro football is not the complicated game some coaches paint it to be.

Take the case of Karl Baldischwiler, a 6 foot 5 inch, 260 pound offensive tackle out of Oklahoma who, for the past five seasons, played for the Detroit Lions. He appeared in all 73 games during that period, 68 as a starter.

Last week Baldischwiler became a Colt. Tomorrow night he will start at tackle against the Oilers in Houston in the Colts' exhibition opener. So much for all that time required to 'learn the system.'"

🏈

Sports Illustrated, on Barry Switzer, Oklahoma coach: "When Barry Switzer want to be charming ... he can persuade wallpaper to leave the wall."

🏈

Beano Cook, ESPN analyst, after the undefeated University of Virginia lost to Georgia Tech and was knocked out of first place in the ACC: "This is the worst thing to happen in Virginia since Appomattox."

🏈

ESPN analyst Bill Curry, during the Penn State-Indiana game (2000) after a terrific block by a pulling guard: "That's one of those Susan B. Anthony blocks—they look like a quarter, but are worth a dollar."

🏈

Grantland Rice, legendary sports writer on winning: "And when that One Great Scorer comes to mark against your name He writes not that you won or lost—But how you played the game."

🏈

Phil Jackman, *Baltimore Evening Sun* sports columnist: "Great bumper stickers showing up in Dallas this week leading up to today's Texas (5-0)—Southern Methodist (5-0) shootout: 'The Lies of Texas are upon you' and 'Support Pro Football: Watch the SMU Mustangs.'"

Bernie Miklasz, *Baltimore News American* sports reporter: "The Colts have slipped to 23rd in the league's defensive rankings. If the musket-carrying foot soldiers at Bunker Hill would have played this brand of defense, we'd be paying homage to kings and queens."

Charlie Jones, NBC play-by-play announcer describing a play during the Dolphins-Colts game: "It's 3rd and 19 on their own 10, McMillan (Baltimore FB) gets the ball ... he's not too thrilled."

Merle Harmon, NBC play-by-play announcer, on Larry Kinnebreu, the Cincinnati Bengals 250 pound FB: "Larry Kinnebreu ran into is own blocker on that play. That might be the hardest that blocker was hit all year."

Phil Wood, WCBM-Radio (Baltimore) sports reporter regarding a disputed play which deprived the Colts of a touchdown: "It's a play that will live in infamy—at least until next week."

John Madden, on the handicap of being small: "The only time they talk about someone being 'too small' is when he isn't very good."

Vito Stellino, *Baltimore Sun* sports reporter, on the charge by a former player that Don Shula fixed Super Bowl III: "It was a little like accusing Thomas Dewey of fixing his loss to Harry Truman in 1948."

Pat Buchanan, columnist and political commentator: "The selection of Geraldine Ferraro for Vice President was, for Walter Mondale, like a Hail Mary pass."

Howard Cosell asking incredulously about the Dallas Cowboys being behind the Washington Redskins, 22-3: "When was the last time you'd seen the Dallas Cowboys in such disarray?

Don Meredith: 'The last time they were in Washington.'" (P.S. The Cowboys won 31-30.)

Chris Thomas, WBAL-TV (Baltimore) sports announcer, on the Colts' defense against the Jets: "Up until yesterday the defense had been more generous than the United Way."

Lou Holtz, highly-regarded coach and astute color analyst, on why he started two Freshman on defense who had been playing Tailback: "Hey, if the Titanic is going down, I'm not going to be playing the piano."

John Madden, CBS color commentator during a pre-season game between the Cowboys and the Oilers: "From the waist down, Earl Campbell has the biggest legs I've even seen on a running back."

Vito Stellino, *Baltimore Sun* sports reporter on Baltimore's effort to bring back the Colts: "Colts lawyers have shown a better prevent defense than the football team did on the field in recent years, but Baltimore has finally penetrated that defense and can start its offense in court."

Phil Jackman, *Baltimore Evening Sun* columnist, describing Denver's winning touchdown in the Broncos' 1983 last minute victory over Baltimore: "On the Broncs' winning score, a Colt safety lined up in the wrong spot, then compounded the error by turning the wrong way (toward Mecca for forgiveness?)."

Renowned sports writer Red Smith, on a football team's record: "They underwhelmed ten opponents, overwhelmed one, and whelmed the other."

Chapter 19

Vito Stellino, *Baltimore Sun* sports reporter on Vince Ferragamo's "spaciness": "There's nothing wrong with having a space cadet as quarterback as long as he gets into orbit."

Ken Murray, *Baltimore Evening Sun* columnist commenting on the problems of Baltimore offensive line coach, Hal Hunter: "There were bodies to the left of him, bodies to the right of him, bodies all over the place. He must have felt like the last man at the Alamo."

Randy Cross, NBC analyst, during the New England-Pittsburgh game, describing a Patriot lineman's vain attempt to catch the Steelers' nifty QB, Kordell Stewart: "It's like trying to catch a Ferrari with a VW Beetle."

John Madden, TV analyst, on John Elway: "He's an immediate cure for coach's burnout."

Dick Enberg, NBC sportscaster, as a Richard Todd pass hit a Jet receiver, ricocheted and was caught by a teammate for a long gain: "Wow! It's great to be good, but it sure doesn't hurt to be lucky."

Bob Costas, NBC sportscaster quoting an unidentified Tampa Bay player about his team's 11-0 loss in the first week of play: "Well, there are 28 teams in the NFL. Last week 12 of them lost and 12 of them won."

Alan Goldstein, *Baltimore Sun* sports reporter, about the 49ers respected coach Bill Walsh: "For the next weeks Bill Walsh will be in full pursuit of another Super Bowl. You will not hear him utter a single mention of 'burnout.' San Francisco just can't stand another fire."

Phil Stone, NBC sportscaster, during the Baltimore-Cleveland game with the Browns leading 38-23: "The temperature is falling - - the hopes of the Colts had already fallen."

Keith Jackson, ABC sportscaster, during the Ohio State-Oklahoma game: "Byars (Ohio State TB) is so big and strong, you have to tackle him in volleys."

Bill Kurtis, upon hearing allegations of drug abuse by the Chargers in 1974: "The way the Chargers played, the drug must have been formaldehyde."

Bob Costas, NBC play-by-play commentator, describing the Pittsburgh Steelers' defensive effort: "The Steelers hold a team meeting on Muncie's body."

Don Meredith, after watching Lynn Swann make a sensational one-handed catch for a 35-yard gain: "Wow, what a pair of hand that guy's got."

Howard Cosell and Don Meredith, during the Monday Night Washington Redskins-San Diego Chargers game: *Cosell:* "Starkey is upset that his alma mater, Columbia, lost to Holy Cross 77-28."

Meredith: "I guess they spent too much time working on offense."

Laura Charles, *Baltimore Sun* "Eyes Only" columnist, about Baltimore City State's Attorney Kurt Schmoke, a former quarterback, who led his alumni team to victory over rival Poly in their annual touch football game, as he scored a TD and threw for another: "It's good to know we have a State's Attorney at the helm who's as good at offense as defense."

Bob Trumpy, NBC football color commentator, following an Eagles' touchdown during the Philadelphia-Baltimore game: "It's very quiet in the stadium, even though the Eagles just scored—waiting for spring training, maybe?"

Alex Hawkins, former Baltimore Colt and later a color commentator: "Big plays are made by big players."

Writer Larry Merchant on football diagrams: "A football play diagram has about as much relationship to what goes on in the field as a diagram of a dance step has to Fred Astaire's dancing on the stage."

Tom Brookshier, TV analyst, after a hugh pile-up on the goal line: "It'll take the *Star Spangled Banner* to get them on their feet."

Phil Jackman, *Baltimore Evening Sun* sports columnist: "Someone asked the famed Doctor of Inside Sports if Bubba Smith and Bubba Baker are related and he replied: 'Absolutely, they're step-bubbas.'"

Syndicated columnist Carl T. Rowan characterizing the political philosophy of Representative Jack Kemp (R, N. Y.), former Buffalo Bills' quarterback: "As conservatives go, Mr. Kemp is more unbending that a Redskins' linebacker."

Dick Enberg, NBC sportscaster, after 270-lb. Chris Ward, Jets' tackle, married the daughter of the heralded Jim Brown: "The Division I scouts are already lining up for the first child."

Kevin Cowherd, *Baltimore Evening Sun* sports columnist, describing Frank Kush's first win ever as an NFL coach: "First, came a smile from the Colts' head coach you wanted to press between the pages of a book."

Pro football writer, on hearing an offensive lineman had to miss the first half because of over-indulging at a Baskins-Robbins: "It proves what can happen on any given sundae."

Dick Enberg, NBC sports play-by-play announcer, on speedy receiver, Roger Carr: "There's a Carr that can really motor."

🏈

Jim Jackson *Baltimore Sun* sports reporter, on Navy's great running back, Napoleon McCallum: "He runs like a deer and cuts like a rabbit."

🏈

Alan Goldstein, *Baltimore Sun* sports reporter on the Colts search for a fleet end: "The search for a 'sleeper' in the receiving corps has uncovered no unexpected treasures. [But] Boss Irsay has been closeted in the film room the past few weeks grading rival receivers for possible purchase or trade. It took Cecil B. DeMille less time to film 'The Ten Commandments.'"

🏈

Carl Ortman, Caltec (Channel 10) TV football play-by-play announcer responding to his partner's comment that, "The quarterback is displaying the intelligence of a higher order": "Besides that, he's awfully smart."

🏈

Phil Wood, *WCBM* Radio sportscaster commenting on the number of new players on the Baltimore Colts football team: "When they open the season, the ball players will be wearing name tags saying, 'Hello, my name is _____.'"

🏈

Vince Bagli, *WBAL*-TV (Baltimore) sports reporter: "Well, the teams have been selected for the Liberty Bowl. Hmm. They ought to play this one in the Vatican—it's Notre Dame against the Jesuit Boston College."

🏈

Cameron Snyder, *Baltimore Sun* sports writer, describing John Riggins' less than glorious performance in a pre-season game against the Miami Dolphins: "John Riggins, usually a rolling stone, just gathered moss in seven first-half rushes for a measly 15 yards."

🏈

Bernie Miklasz, *Baltimore News American* sports writer predicting what will happen at the New Orleans-Philadelphia game: "Bum Phillips and Marion Campbell get to exchange corn pone recipes after the game."

🏈

Scott Garceau, *WMAR*-TV (Baltimore) sports director: "The Houston Oilers haven't won since Moby Dick was a minnow."

🏈

Phil Jackman, *Baltimore Evening Sun* sports columnist, on the cancellation of the Beach Boys concert: "Originally, the Beach Boys were supposed to concert following the Colt-Patriots game tomorrow so Foxboro wouldn't look like a ghost town. Then it was announced the proper arrangements couldn't be made and the show was off. But that ain't the way we heard it. Word is that the singers, no spring chickens, were afraid they would be pressed into service as the right side of Baltimore's offensive line if they showed their faces."

🏈

Vito Stellino, *Baltimore Sun* sports reporter, on Bubba Smith's allegations regarding Super Bowl III in which the Colts lost to the N.Y. Jets, 16-7: "It's difficult to seriously discuss Smith's charge. I can't wait for his book revealing that the Civil War was fixed to unite America."

🏈

Chapter 20

Bernie Miklasz, *Baltimore News American* sports reporter, on the Colts loss to Miami, 37-0: "The Colts chartered plane touched down safely on the return trip to Baltimore-Washington airport Sunday night. It was the only Colt touchdown of the day."

Lee Corso, TV analyst, during the Nebraska-Penn State football game: "Tom Osborne [of Nebraska] is the E. F. Hutton of football. When he speaks, people listen."

Reporter, relating the story Al Davis heard about Nicky Hilton, that he (Hilton) had made a quick $100,000 in Los Angeles baseball: "It was his brother not him. And it was San Diego, not L. A. and football, not baseball. And $1 million, not $100,000. And he didn't make it, he lost it."

Bernie Miklasz, *Baltimore News American* sportswriter, predicting the outcome of the New England-Los Angeles Rams game: "If this one ends in a tie, the Hannah brothers—John (Patriots) and Charley (Rams)—will settle it with an arm-wrestling contest."

Tom Brookshier, CBS analyst, following a measurement for first down: "Fourth and inches to go! The War of 1812 was lost over less than that."

Bob Trumpy, NBC football analyst: "If it weren't for bad luck, Baltimore wouldn't have any luck at all."

Tom Brookshier to his announcing partner, Pat Summeral, during a timeout called to allow a player to change his jersey: "All of our shirts used to be stitched, didn't they, Pat?"

Summeral: "Yeah, with blow-out patches."

Chuck Thompson, *WCBM* football play-by-play announcer: "The way the Colts have been playing lately, it's going to get late awfully early."

Bill Fleming, ABC sports announcer, quoting Tom Osborne, Nebraska coach: "A team usually makes its greatest improvement between its first and second games. I hope we're better against Wyoming than we were against Penn State." (Nebraska beat Penn State, 44-6)

A reporter's response when asked who he thought would win a personality contest between Bud Grant and Tom Landry: "It would be a tie for second place."

John Steadman, *Baltimore News American* sports editor, after visiting the Colts training camp: "The Holiday Inn in Anderson, Indiana, where the Indianapolis Colts are training, serves an exotic beverage called a 'Colt Kicker'—drink two and you think you're Raul Allegre (Colts' kicker)."

Frank Glieber, CBS sportscaster, when Mike Moroski, Atlanta Falcons' reserve quarterback replaced Steve Bartkowski, who was out with strained knee ligaments: "He doesn't have Bartkowski's arm—but then he doesn't have Bartkowski's legs either."

Ken Murray, *Baltimore Evening Sun* sportswriter, on the Colts' back-to-back losses to Miami and Cleveland: "The last two Sundays, the Colts were slapped around by a rookie named Marino and a surgeon named Sipe."

Bernie Miklasz, *Baltimore News American* sports writer on how the Colts Jeff Hart would play against the Jets' Mark Gastineau, the defensive end noted for his dancing antics: "Hart will attempt to remove Gastineau's dancing shoes on Sunday."

🏈

Mark Whicker, *Philadelphia Daily News* sports columnist on the durability of NFL backs: "Dorsett went on to say that Eric Dickerson has a chance to be as durable as he has been because, 'He's got that elusive quality.' But no one can be sure. The typical NFL running back is a meteor . . Sixteen tons, sixteen games and what do you get? Another day in the trainer's room, for starters."

🏈

Bob Chandler, NBC analyst on why Cleveland Browns' Mike Pruit was running so hard against the Baltimore Colts: "He doesn't want Jim Brown to come out of retirement."

🏈

Sam DeLuca, TV analyst, on Ray Guy's towering punts: "Anything that goes up that high and travels that far ought to have a stewardess on it."

🏈

Sports reporter to smug coach who looked at a crowded meeting of football mentors and asked, "How many great coaches do you think there are in this room?": *Reporter:* "One less than you think."

🏈

Sign at the Army-Notre Dame game: "We were underdogs on D-Day, too."

🏈

Dick Vermeil, CBS analyst, about Wendell Tyler, when he was traded from the Rams to the 49ers: "Wendell Tyler scored a touchdown every 20th time he got the ball. Of course, he fumbled it every 19th time."

🏈

Vince Scully, TV sportscaster, on statistics: "Statistics are used like a drunk uses a lamp post—for support, not illumination."

🏈

Frank Glieber, CBS announcer, on the condition of Atlanta quarterback Steve Bartkowski's knees: "Bartkowski's knees are really scarred after all those operations. He looks as if he's been in a knife fight with a midget."

Phil Jackman, *Baltimore Evening Sun* columnist, on Cleveland: "Even a sportswriter friend who lived and worked there for years says, 'Putting a dome stadium in Cleveland would be like putting earrings on a pig.'"

Bernie Miklasz, *Baltimore News American* sportswriter, on the Rose Bowl game between U.C.L.A. and Illinois: "The Julia Child Award goes to the cook whose gourmet dish caused nine U.C.L.A. players to come down with food poisoning the day before the Rose Bowl. Food for thought: So why was it Illinois put forth the sickening performance?"

Bob Ryan, on Lindsey Nelson's preference for wild sport jackets: "Lindsey has never let success go to his clothing."

Ken Murray, *Baltimore Evening Sun* sportswriter, indicating with the appropriate headline that the Houston Oilers' problem was the "teams collective paunch": "Studley [interim coach Chuck Studley] indicates Oilers Problem is a Weighty One."

Bill Tanton, *Baltimore Evening Sun* columnist, on playing for a win or a tie: "On the subject of playing to win or going for a tie, didn't Penn State's Joe Paterno say it all when he commented, 'If I'm having brain surgery, I'll be damned if I want that surgeon playing for a tie!'"

Ken Murray, Baltimore Evening Sun sportswriter, quoting Brian Sipe, Cleveland quarterback, on continued reports of his dead throwing arm: "You guys [the media] are great for me. You make me feel like an over-achiever whenever I do something good."

Merlin Olsen, TV analyst, on Cliff Branch, after he caught a pass in traffic, eluded three tacklers, and ran out of bounds to stop the clock prior to halftime: "Cliff Branch—he's so elusive, it's like trying to catch a butterfly."

Alex Hawkins, TV analyst, on records: "Records are goals not monuments."

Jim Nantz, CBS' sportscaster, on the Dallas Cowboys coach, Jimmy Johnson: "The only time Jimmy didn't run up the score was 27 years ago when he took the SAT."

Alan Goldstein, *Baltimore Sun* sports reporter, on mismatches: "Recently, former Navy mentor Rick Forzano recalled how it felt to play a tackling dummy for some of the nation's 'semi-pro' teams. He remembered playing Notre Dame and wondering why it took so many charter buses to transport the Irish. 'Then I watched them load up,' Forzano said. 'Five of their lineman filled one bus.'"

A Houston newsman on Earl Campbell's unselfishness and generosity toward his teammates: "If it were up to Earl, he'd change the name of the "I" to the "We."

Dick Vermeil, CBS analyst, commenting on a missed field goal attempt by the Tampa Bay Buccaneers: "Low and outside. Ball four."

Dick Vermeil, CBS analyst, after Green Bay's oft-injured quarterback Lynn Dickey ran the ball: "Dickey is not the man you want running the ball. He's been hurt so many times, he should wear a Red Cross on his jersey."

Chapter 21

Dick Enberg, NBC sportscaster, after the Seattle Seahawks' Don Doornink scored: "He has a brother and a father who are physicians and he will be back at medical school after this season. Well, he had a good prescription for that touchdown."

❦

John Steadman, *Baltimore News American* sports editor, on the tough, mean defensive ends that sparked the Baltimore Colts to the 1958 and 1959 NFL championships: "The Colts' ends always justified the means."

❦

Ken Murray, *Baltimore Evening Sun* sportswriter, on how Coach Tom Flores, celebrated his Super Bowl victory over the Redskins: "He went to a private party for about 2,000 intimate friends. Enroute to the party, Flores tried to dissuade linebacker Matt Millen from ripping a window off the bus in which they were riding. 'Matt, don't do it,' Flores said. Millen said, 'I'm getting sick.' Flores said, 'OK, do it.'"

❦

Lee Corso, TV analyst, about Johnnie Jones, the Tennessee Vols running back: "There's only one ball, so you may as well give it to Jones. He's their best back."

❦

Sportswriter Jimmy Cannon on Howard Cosell: "If Howard Cosell was a sport, it would be Roller Derby."

❦

CBS analyst Steve Davis, during the 1983 "Blue-Gray" game, when defensive tackle Michael Gunner and two other linemen threw a "Blue" back for a 5-yard loss on a counter play: "Looks like Michael Gunner called a board meeting in the backfield."

❦

Dick Enberg, NBC sportscaster, on Lester Hayes, L. A. Raiders' defensive back: "Lester Hayes is big on talking about deceased Presidents—72,000 worth of them. This represents the amount of money the winner of the Super Bowl will receive."

●

Bill Glauber, *Baltimore Sun* sportswriter, eliciting a response from Wake Forest coach, Al Groh, after the University of Maryland edged his Demon Deacons, 36-33 in the last seconds: *Groh:* "It was just another Wake Forest-Maryland game where the score looks like the top of a pinball machine."

●

Vince Bagli, *WBAL*-TV (Baltimore) Sports Director on losing: "It's tough—no one knows what to say in the loser's room."

●

Repartee between broadcasting team of Pat Summerall and John Madden when John Riggins threw a pass to end Charlie Brown during Redskins-49ers game: *Madden:* "Who would've expected a 'Hog' to throw the football."

Summerall: "Why wouldn't you expect a 'Hog' to throw it? It's a pigskin."

●

Vito Stellino, *Baltimore Sun* sports writer, about the Colts-Browns game: "The Colts and Cleveland Browns will match goose eggs today, and the worry for the Colts is they may wind up getting scrambled."

●

Dick Vermeil, CBS analyst, describing a hard-working player: "He stands tall as an over-achieving, under-achiever."

●

Bill Tanton, *Baltimore Evening Sun* sports columnist, on Tom Osborne and Nebraska football: "He coaches in a state where the university's sports information director once said, 'The most important thing in this state is Nebraska football. The second most important thing is Nebraska spring football.'"

●

Mike Klingamon, *Baltimore Evening Sun* sportswriter, querying Gino Marchetti, Baltimore's great defensive end, on his football career: *Marchetti:* "If the good Lord came down to me and said, 'Gino, would you rather play football until you're 65 for $20,000 a year, or go into business and make $150,000?,' I'd pick football. Is it a wise choice? No, but it's a happy one."

🏈

Len Berman, NBC sports anchor, while showing hi-lites of the Nebraska-Miami Orange Bowl in 1984: "Bernie Kosar (QB) threw for the first touchdown to Stanley Shakespeare. Hmm. With a name like that, Shakespeare must write his own plays in the huddle."

🏈

Brent Musburger, CBS sports, on the Redskins' Joe Theismann's volubility: "Joe never met a microphone he didn't like."

🏈

Frank Gifford, ABC sportscaster, explaining Howard Cosell's absence at the Dinah Shore classic banquet: "The weather was so nice in New York that Howard went to the park to feed the pigeons—to the cats."

🏈

Al Michaels and Lee Grosscup, ABC broadcasting team, in a discussion during the 1983 Army-Navy game: *Michaels:* "Army and Navy came to Hollywood and who do you think is the referee—a man by the name of Vincent Price."

Grosscup: "Yes and fittingly, both teams are playing the 'Monster' defense."

🏈

Howard Cosell, on mistakes: "No matter what the sport, it's mistakes that beat you."

🏈

NBC analyst Bob Griese, on the Super Bowl: "The trouble is the writers and television people spend two weeks building the game up and the next four weeks tearing it down."

🏈

Frank Glieber, CBS sportscaster, describing 49ers quarterback Joe Montana eluding the Lions' defensive linemen: "It's amazing what the human body can do when pursued by a larger human body."

🏈

Pat Hayden, CBS analyst, anticipating a punt on fourth down in the Cotton Bowl: "Would you be concerned if your punt returner was named Jitters?"

🏈

Dick Enberg, NBC sportscaster, about kicker Chris Bahr, after he had kicked a field goal: "Chris Bahr's wife had read about him before she met him. But she said she read so much about the 'much-maligned Chris Bahr,' she thought his first name was 'much-maligned.'"

🏈

Frank Gifford, after Jerry Rice of the 49ers flew by the San Diego secondary and scored on a long TD pass: "They looked like they were waiting to ask him for an autograph."

🏈

Lee Corso, TV analyst, commenting during the pre-game show, as one parachutist landed on the 50-yard line following his partner's landing on the 30-yard line: "This guy is the first team."

🏈

CBS broadcasting team Frank Glieber and Dick Vermeil, discussing a crucial call: *Glieber:* "They're on the five and John McKay has got a decision to make—go for it or try for a field goal."
Vermeil: "The field goal kicker made the decision on his last attempt—when he missed."

🏈

Jim Brinson, *WJZ*-TV (Baltimore) sportscaster, during the Robert Irsay-Arizona caper: "I just flew in from Arizona—and boy are my arms tired."

🏈

CBS play-by-play announcer Don Criqui during the Baltimore-Jacksonville game, when it began raining: "Here in Florida it rains twice a week—first for four days and then for three days."

🏈

Don Meredith and Howard Cosell, during ABC's "Monday Night Football": *Meredith:* "The pass is going to set up the run."
Cosell: "If that's not true, you've got a scoop."

🏈

Tony Kornheiser, *Washington Post* News Service, about Joe Theismann as a media performer: "Theismann can do 15 minutes on a wrong number. When you reach out and touch Joe, bring your lunch. Some people speak in sentences. Some people even speak in paragraphs. Theismann speaks in mini-series. He walks into a movie theater, sees the red exit light, assumes it's a live camera and does a 'lounge act.'"

Two sportswriters debating the merits of the modern football players versus the stars of the yesteryear: *Sportswriter #1:* "Okay, how many yards per game would Jim Thorpe average against the big defensive monsters of today?"

Sportswriter #2: "Oh, maybe 100-125 yards a game."

Sportswriter #1: "What's so great about that?"

Sportswriter #2: "Well, you've got to remember, Thorpe would be 96 years old!"

Alan Goldstein, *Baltimore Sun* reporter, on coaching vacancies: "Defections by top-rank coaches soon became a household gag. When the surviving NFL coaches posed for a group portrait last March, minus eight casualties from the previous year, Tampa Bay's John McKay cracked, 'It looks like a World War II bombing raid. How many of us got back?'"

Kevin Cowherd, *Baltimore Evening Sun* columnist, on Al Davis: "Maybe it was Hunter Thompson, the gonzo journalist and author, who first alerted me to the bizarre potential of the Raiders. Thompson had an opportunity to interview the iconoclastic owner Al Davis [who] showed up in his usual uniform: dark sunglasses, black leather jacket, dark jeans, with a menacing sneer that spoke volumes of tough upbringing in the streets of Brooklyn. Thompson wrote: 'Al Davis makes Darth Vader look like a wimp.'"

Dick Vermeil, CBS analyst, on Atlanta receiver, Stacey Bailey: "I'm not saying Stacey Bailey is thin—but he's built like that yard marker."

Chapter 22

John Eisenberg, *Baltimore Sun* sports columnist, on the Ravens' 37-0 loss to Pittsburgh: "Actually, don't put much of the blame on the defense, which didn't play badly considering that the offense seemed intent on filming its version of a Marx Brothers comedy."

Alan Goldstein, *Baltimore Sun* reporter on Eric Dickerson of the Rams: "When a reporter asked him to name the backs he most admired, he ticked off the names Brown, Simpson, Sayers, and Payton. 'And I assume you'd like to included in that list one day?' he was asked. 'Yeah at the top,' Dickerson replied."

Don Criqui, NBC sportscaster, during the Colts-Patriots game, on why Baltimore's Curtis Dickey would score if he got a step on the defense: "There are four people in the world faster than Curtis Dickey and none of them play for the New England Patriots."

Frank Gifford-Howard Cosell exchange during ABC's Monday Night Football: *Cosell:* "There will be a veritable plethora of turn-overs."
Gifford: "Yes, Howard, and there will also be many of them."

Ken Murray, *Baltimore Evening Sun* columnist, describing the exchange between quarterback Ken Stabler (New Orleans) and half-back Walter Payton (Chicago) after Payton threw two touchdowns against the Saints: *Stabler:* "Don't you go passing the ball. They'll make you a quarterback."
Payton: "Not me. Quarterbacks don't make enough money."

Kevin Cowherd, *Baltimore Evening Sun* columnist, on Super Bowl hype: "Clearly, we're talking serious hype here. We're talking a football game turned into the Normandy invasion. 'How do you deal with it?' defensive tackle Dave Butz was saying. 'I'll tell you. I can see a lot of times where you'd be forced to eat in your room.'"

Reggie Rucker, NBC analyst, on Houston's failure to move the ball against the Indianapolist Colts: "The Oilers are in their tango offense —1, 2, 3 kick."

Bernie Miklasz, *Baltimore New American* sports writer, on John Elway: "Two weeks ago John Elway missed a game because of the flu. Just think about that. Here's a guy who said he didn't want to play in Baltimore because of the weather."

Len Berman, NBC sports anchor, commenting on the intense rivalry of the teams, prior to the 1984 Pittsburgh-Oakland game: "This is the first game where a penalty flag will be dropped in the parking lot."

Kevin Cowherd, *Baltimore Evening Sun* columnist, commenting on Joe Theismann's explanation of how he deals with Super Bowl hype, "You deal with hype by telling yourself this: This is what I worked for.": "Of course, Theismann admits he never met a camera, micro-phone or notepad he didn't like so maybe his opinion must be taken lightly."

Jeff Gordon, *Baltimore News American* staff, after the Redskins clobbered the L. A. Rams in NFC semi-finals: "Now the Rams know how George McGovern felt in 1972 [a 520-17 beating in the Electoral College]. That was the political equivalent of having your spleen removed with a pick ax."

Mike Patrick, ABC-TV play-by-play man, during the Vikings-Giants wild card play-off game (12/27/97): "Roman Orben is one-on-one with the Vikings' John Randle. He better pack a lunch. It's going to be a long day."

♠

Tom Brookshier, CBS analyst, during the telecast of the New Orleans-Philadelphia football game, following a promotional spot for a Louisville-North Carolina State basketball game: "Denny Crum always has a great team at Louisville. They have a collective IQ of about 40, but they can play basketball."

♠

Phil Jackman, *Baltimore Evening Sun* columnist, about CBS football analyst, Tom Brookshier and his remark: (see previous quote) "The combined IQ of the Louisville basketball team is 40."
—and—
"Last Sunday, in Philly, the Eagles retired Brookshier's number—40—and somebody kiddingly asked before the ballgame if the 40 referred to Tom's uniform or IQ. The line obviously stuck in the ex-player's mind."
—and—
"So what's the big deal about Tom Brookshier's crack about the University of Louisville's basketball team having a combined IQ of 40? For years on regional and national telecasts, we've been listening to crowds chant, 'If you can't go to college go to State,' about North Carolina State."
—and—
"Had your irony today? Guess who's going to be the keynote speaker at Louisville's football banquet next season. Of course, Tom (the combined IQ of the Louisville basketball team in 40) Brookshier."

♠

Blackie Sherrod, *Dallas Times Herald* columnist, after noting that the Cowboys had been put on the market for a price tag of $60 million, added that a friend indicated this included the cheerleaders: "But if you want the cheerleader's costumes, that'll be another seven bucks."

♠

James Lofton, NBC analyst, about the Tennessee Oilers passing game during the Oilers-Ravens game: "For as much as QB Steve McNair goes to the wide receivers they could be in the witness protection program."

♠

Bernie Miklasz, *Baltimore News American* sports writer, on Colt back-up quarterback Mark Hermann: "Mark Hermann is built like Raggedy Andy. And when he drops back to pass ever so sloooowly, grass has been know to grow through his cleats."

●

Carl Ortman, *KBL*-TV, Channel 10 (Baltimore) announcer, during a high school game, in which the team behind by a score of 28-13 called a time-out with one second to go: "Well, here comes that fifteen-point play."

●

Vito Stellino, *Baltimore Sun* reporter, on Boomer Esiason's complaint that he was not selected A.C.C. player of the year and failed to receive other honors: "I had to laugh when he [Esiason] announced there's no 'politics' in the NFL. There's more politics in the NFL than you'll see at one of the national conventions."

●

Mike Klingamon, *Baltimore Evening Sun* sports writer, on the aftermath of the famous 1958 Colt-Giants sudden-death game win by Baltimore, 23–17: "When the hubbub subsided, Myrha and Mutscheller decided to strut around town in their Colt jackets with white sleeves. 'Then we walked into Hutzler's (a department store) and found a whole rack of them,' says Myrha."

●

Phil Jackman, *Baltimore Evening Sun* columnist, on Joe Don Looney: "It turns out that an identity crisis was the only problem Joe Don Looney ever had. The former Colt from Oklahoma says, 'Life has always been a Catch-22 for me. After all, all I ever wanted to be was God.'"

●

Marvin Raphael, on the two minute offense: "The best way to kill an hour is to watch the 49ers two-minute offense."

●

Bernie Miklasz, *Baltimore News American* sportswriter, about the Baltimore Colt's defensive line: "A strange group. At left end Donnell Thompson played like Godzilla on some Sundays and like Casper the Friendly Ghost on others."

●

Bob Maisel, *Baltimore Sun* columnist, responding to a fan's view that Raymond Berry, former All-pro offensive end with the Colts, would not even be able to play in the league today: "Horse feathers! Hogwash! The day they devise a game that Raymond Berry can't play it won't be football."

John Madden, former coach and now a TV analyst: "Miami coach, Don Shula, makes the whole better than the parts."

Joe Terranova in *Sports Illustrated*, evaluating the University of Georgia: "The Bulldogs main recruiting goal in 1984 was to perk up the offense and Maxwell House couldn't have done it better."

Phil Mushnick, TV critic, on the broadcasting style of Phyllis George: "She talks to the viewers like she's the next step after toilet training."

Indianapolis, Indiana, sports columnist after the Baltimore Colts were moved from the Monumental City to Indianapolis, under cover of darkness by the Mayflower moving company: "Now that the Mayflower has landed, it remains to be seen whether it carried a load of turkeys."

Lee Corso, former coach and currently a TV analyst, on what to do against a super defensive lineman: "If he's big, strong, and fast, run right at him. If he's big, strong, fast, and mean, call a time-out."

Boston *Globe* sports writer Dan Shaughnessy, after watching Boston College drive to Notre Dame's 4 yard line, where Mike Cloud was given the ball on four straight downs but failed to punch it into the end zone for the winning TD: "They needed 4 yards to win. They got 3 yards and a dust of Cloud."

Steve Kornacki of the *Ann Arbor News* (Michigan), on why he would love to see Louis Lipps, a wide receiver from Southern Mississippi, selected in the first round by the Steelers, break free and score a game-winning touchdown to beat Jackie Shipp, an Oklahoma linebacker, who was a first-round pick of the Miami Dolphins: "Then, newspapers around the country can run the headline: "Loose Lipps Sinks Shipp.""

Chapter 23

Hank Stram, CBS analyst, describing the Giants' fine running back, Joe Morris: "He has great leg drive. It's important to have leg drive. You can't fire a cannon out of a canoe."

Grantland Rice, famous sports writer on Notre Dame's "Four Horsemen": "Outlined against the blue-gray October sky, the Four Horsemen rode again. In dramatic lore they were known as famine, pestilence, destruction, and death. These are only aliases. Their real names are Stuhldreher, Miller, Crowley, and Layden. They formed the crest of the South Bend cyclone."

Chris Thomas, *WBAL*-TV (Baltimore) sportscaster, on some of the Communist women who could never pass a sex test: "There's a runner in East Germany—well, if she came to this country, George Allen would offer her a try-out."

Brent Musburger, ABC play-by-play commentator, after Florida State's third team QB Marcus Outzen, led his team to a 23-12 victory over Florida: "Well, his nickname if Rooster—and today he's got something to crow about."

Johnny Holliday and Jack Scarbath, University of Maryland radio play-by-play man and analyst respectively, discussing the Terps speedy receiver Azizuddin Abdur Ra'oof, following his catch and 55 yard run for a touchdown: *Holliday:* "What a catch—and did he move out!"

Scarbath: "Yes—he was in the end zone before you could pronounce his name."

Roy Firestone, ESPN analyst during the Minnesota-Chicago Sunday Night game: "So many players of the Vikings have been involved with the police, the team picture next year will have to be taken from the front and side."

Former NFL kicker Jesse Atkinson, on trying to figure out how many kickers shuttle in and out of professional football training camps: "It can be like trying to figure out how many marriages a diva has."

Michael Olesker, *Baltimore Sun* columnist, on the NFL-USFL trial: "A jury of six people in New York City, none of whom knows a blocked punt from a blocked urethra, decided the National Football League had violated the antitrust laws of America . . ."

Don Criqui, NBC play-by-play announcer, relating a story from a Mark Gastineau roast: "Gastineau was asked to spell Mississippi. He asked, 'What to you mean—the river or the state?"

Don Criqui, relating a story from a Mark Gastineau roast: "I'm not saying he's cheap, but one day he pulled a $5 bill out of his wallet and Lincoln blinked from being exposed to the light."

TNT commentator, Pat Hayden, after broadcaster Skip Caray said Chicago's 38-9 rout of L. A. was surprising because the Rams were an emotional team: "The guys at the Alamo were emotional too, and it didn't do them much good."

John Steadman, *Baltimore Evening Sun* columnist quoting Howard "Red" Grange, the "Galloping Ghost," on why he didn't play golf: "Golf is as boring as kicking extra points."

Dick Enberg, NBC play-by-play announcer, on William Perry: "William Perry—'the 'Refrigerator'—was asked how much he weighed when he was born. He replied, 'I was 13 ? lbs. I was born on December 13, 14, 15.'"

George Allen, CBS analyst and former coach, about the Atlanta Falcons: "Waiting for Atlanta to win a championship is like leaving the porch light on for Jimmy Hoffa."

Marv Albert, NBC play-by-play announcer characterizing Brian Bosworth, the highly publicized Seattle linebacker: "The man with the most recognized Mohawk since the French and Indian War."

Tim Brant, ABC-TV analyst during the Rose Bowl game between Purdue and Washington: "Purdue's Montrell Love has such fast feet, when he runs it's like dancing on a light bulb."

Bob Griese, former Miami QB, now an NBC analyst, about the Jets' Joe Klecko: "Going against him is like playing chess with boxing gloves."

Beano Cook, sports commentator: "The two most important jobs in America are held by foreigners—room service and field-goal kicking."

Mel Proctor, WTBS announcer: "The University of Wisconsin has a Lawrence Welk offense—a one, a two, a three, 'n' a punt."

Bob Costas, host of NBC's "NFL Live" show, explaining to Paul Maguire how he was able to predict how an NFL team would position its middle linebacker: "As Magic Johnson once said, 'It's as if I have ESPN.'"

John Madden, incomparable CBS-TV colorcaster, during a sideline close-up of Minnesota Vikings' Coach Jerry Burns: "Jerry Burns looks like he just came out of the dryer."

NBC play-by-play announcer, Dick Enberg, obviously impressed with the Pittsburgh Steelers' effective trapping game: "Trap, trap, trap! These Steelers—they'd trap an usher."

Dick Vermeil, former Philadelphia Eagles' coach and a TV color-caster, during the Blue-Gray All Star game, about QB Neal O'Donnell after the Maryland QB scrambled around and finally threw a TD pass to his tight end: "O'Donnell has 4.9 speed. He comes from a family of 9 kids. Boy, you get to use that speed just getting to the dinner table."

Bill Tammeus, columnist for the *Kansas City Star,* after the Kansas City Chiefs defeated the winless Dallas Cowboys 36-28: "It was nice to see the Chiefs win Sunday, though beating Dallas this year is like knocking off Harold Stassen in a presidential primary."

Bill Walsh, NBC's newest football analyst, describing why a receiv-er failed to catch a pass: "He was looking downfield before he took his eyes off the ball."

Ross Claven, play-by-play announcer for Radio WSBA (York, Pa.), during a game between West York and Dover, commenting on the fine performance of one of the players: "Sweitzer did it all today. He was the big cheese."

Roy Firestone, ESPN colorcaster, on Ron Margerum, L. A. Rams' receiver: "He's good but injuries have held him back. He's had more surgeries than Michael Jackson's chin."

Don Criqui, NBC play-by-play commentator during the Buffalo-Redskins game, about the Bills' great defensive end: "Bruce Smith talks a good game and plays an even better one."

Frank Kush, after the Baltimore Colts suffered a disappointing loss to Cleveland: "We got the 'Drum Award'. Every time they wanted to throw, we got beat."

Jack Buck CBS Radio play-by-play man during the Saints-Vikings play-off game with Minnesota far ahead 31-10: "They call New Orleans the Crescent City, but we might be due for an eclipse."

🏈

Steve Buchance, WTTG-TV (Washington, D.C.) sports announcer, describing a play on a highlight film: "There's Iowa's quarterback, Mark Vlasic, who got out of a pickle, and then threw a touchdown pass."

🏈

Vito Stellino, *Baltimore Sun* sports reporter, on NFL officiating: "Officiating in the NFL is shrouded in more secrecy that the KGB. It's time for glasnost for the men in the striped shirts."

🏈

Stellino again, after the Ravens beat the Bengals: "The lame duck Ravens did some quacking yesterday."

🏈

Sam Rutigliano, CBS sports analyst, noting the referee was on the phone to the replay official in the booth: "Notice he's taking his time—must be a collect call."

🏈

Repartee between John Madden and Pat Summeral: *Madden:* "Joe Montana doesn't run much anymore unless there is a sideline close by." *Summeral:* "Well, I always said he was an intelligent player."

🏈

Paul Maguire, NBC football analyst and former pro football player: "The quarterback definitely isn't the smartest guy on the team. It couldn't be anybody who puts his hands on another guy's behind in public before thousands of people."

🏈

Chapter 24

Phil Jackman, *Baltimore Evening Sun* columnist, in a not-too-veiled reminder about the Baltimore Colts' move to Indianapolis in the dark of night: "The Indianapolis Colts' highlight film might be named (with respect to Clark Gable and Claudette Colbert) 'It Happened One Night.'"

CBS radio announcer Jack Buck, when Chicago's William "Refrigerator" Perry, 300 pounds, tackled New Orleans Saints' runningback "Ironhead" Heyward, 260 pounds: "It looked like sumo wrestling."

Scott Ostler, on why it took five and a half hours to give controversial Patriot end Zeke Mowatt a lie detector test: "The polygraph operator was the same guy who made the decisions on instant replay."

Dick Enberg, NBC play-by-play commentator, about the effective play of Chris Carter and A. C. Carter of the Vikings during the Minnesota-Raiders game: "They're a couple of pills [to the L. A. Raiders] those Carters."

John Feinstein, on the top indicator that an athlete needs a study counselor: When the coach starts including detailed instructions with all new socks."

Commentator Beano Cook on the two things you never bet against: "Russia in winter and Notre Dame in South Bend."

Vito Stellino, *Baltimore Sun* reporter, as he made his selection of the Giants–Jets game: "The battle for New York is being played—where else—in New Jersey."

❦

Comments by play-by-play man Dick Stockton and analyst Joe Theismann during halftime of the Washington-Green Bay game which saw Green Bay play a poor first half: *Theismann:* "I'm not sure what Coach Forrest Gregg told the Packers at halftime. Maybe he told them they were gutless, played without intensity, had poor concentration and were just awful."

Stockton: "Yeah, and they were the nice things he said."

❦

John Eisenberg, *Baltimore Sun* sports columnist, evaluating 1987 Heisman Trophy hopefuls: "Michigan State's Lorenzo White is going to the Rose Bowl, but he's the Heisman's Harold Stassen—always up, never in."

❦

Bob Griese, NBC color analyst, after watching Auburn's tight end catch pass after pass against Syracuse in the Sugar Bowl: "They're going to have to put a box and one on Tillman."

❦

Dick Enberg, NBC play-by-play commentator, describing how the outstanding play by Denver quarterback Mark Haynes frustrated Houston QB Warren Moon: "Haynes has been so effective against the Oilers' receivers, he has reduced Warren to a half moon."

❦

The announcing team of Hank Stram and Jack Buck discussing the use of polaroid shots by pro teams: *Stram:* "Polaroid pictures are used to check the defensive alignments. You know what they say: 'One picture is worth a thousand words.'"

Buck: "Yes. Someone once said to me if a picture is worth a thousand words, why don't you shut up?"

❦

Sam Rutigliano, former coach and later a colorcaster, commenting about a meeting of officials: "Well, another officials huddle! It looks like Reykjavick."

Merlin Olson, NBC color analyst, on why Denver's John Elway deserves the "Insomnia Award": "He's kept more people awake in this league than anyone else trying to figure out how to defend him."

John Madden looking ahead to the 1988 NFC Championship game between Washington and Minnesota: "These teams didn't have a lot of respect coming into the play-offs—it should be called the Rodney Dangerfield Bowl."

Pat Summerall, CBS play-by-play commentator, about one of the toughest defensive positions: "If you're a nose tackle in the dome, you spend a lot of time looking at the rafters."

Pat Summerall, following a lengthy penalty explanation by the referee: "That ties a record by Gerry Seaman for the longest penalty call of the year."

Dan Dierdorf, Monday Nite Football analyst, about Miami's Bernie Parmelee gaining a first down by stretching out with the ball: "Bernie Parmelee, who used to drive a U.P.S. truck, reached out and delivered a first down."

Don Criqui, CBS sports announcer, about the Baltimore Ravens aggressive special teams stalwart, Benny Thompson: "Thompson would go hang gliding in a tornado."

John Madden, CBS football analyst, on John Elway: "He's an immediate cure for coach's burnout."

Pat Summerall, CBS play-by-play sportscaster, on why William Perry "The Refrigerator" is not playing in the Bears' backfield anymore: "The 'Refrigerator' outgrew the kitchen."

Pete Axthelm ridiculing the fact that the N. Y. Jets were a 2-point home-team favorite against the Vikings: "The Jets are the worst home-team since Germany before the Normandy invasion."

Beano Cook, on why a star football player dropped out of college: "He got tired of his dad writing him for money."

Mike Patrick, ESPN play-by-play announcer, commenting on how the Houston Oilers use their tight end, after a rare pass to Chris Verkulst: "Here in Houston they throw to the tight end once a month whether they need it or not."

Dan Jiggets, TV analyst and former Chicago Bears' lineman, about Deion "Prime Time" Sanders, when the rookie cornerback of the Atlanta Falcons ran a kick-off out of bounds after a three yard gain: "You're paid to run the ball upfield. 'Prime Time' just moved to 'Late Night.'"

Bob Trumpy, NBC football analyst, commenting prior to the Bears-Packers game: "These people don't play a football game. It's more like a train wreck."

John Madden on Mike Ditka: "When you turn on your TV set and see Mike Ditka talking calmly to his QB, you know the game hasn't started yet."

Al Michaels, ABC-TV play-by-play announcer, about Walter Payton, following his scintillating fake-filled run against the Green Bay Packers: "Only Ginger Rogers could have stayed with him on that play."

Washington *Times* sports columnist Tom Knott, as the Redskins hit their bye week winless after 7 games: "Two byes would be appropriate. That would make the Redskins the bye-bye team."

MARTIN D. (MITCH) TULLAI

Bob Trumpy, on why he called his fragile Bengal teammate, Pat McNally "Candlelight": "Because one good blow and he was out."

●

Baltimore Sun, headline after the Ravens defeated the Bengals 20-13 and running back Priest Holmes rushed for 227 yards: "Winning is rush for Ravens."

●

Scott Ostler's evaluation of Brian Bosworth's pro football career: "I overslept on Sunday and missed it."

●

Charlie Jones, NBC sportscaster, on Nebraska's secondary in the Fiesta Bowl: "The most inexpensive—uh, inexperienced—part of the defense."

●

Tim Brant, CBS color analyst, during the Notre Dame-Miami game, following Raghib "Rocket" Ishmail's 94 yard kick-off return: "He's quicker than gossip."

●

Keith Mills, WMAR-TV (Baltimore, Md.) sports announcer, about the melee which occurred in the LSU-Florida State game: "There was more action in this game than in the Douglas-Holyfield fight."

●

Don Criqui, NBC play-by-play announcer, commenting on the size of NFL players during the Pittsburgh-Cleveland game: "Some of these guys are so heavy, their pictures fall off the wall."

●

Pat Hayden, color analyst on TNT-TV, describing James Brown, the Eagles' linebacker: "Playing against him is like having a continuous root canal."

●

Skip Caray, play-by-play announcer on TNT-TV during the Houston-Pittsburgh game: "Bubby Brister has a candy bar coming out and Louis Lipps has a cookie coming out—Wow, Zits City!"

●

Kevin Kiley, ESPN colorcaster, about playing Tennessee: "Agreeing to be the opponent in Tennessee's homecoming game is like a turkey agreeing to show up for dinner on Thanksgiving."

Sportswriter to a football player fresh from his hair stylist: "I've seen better haircuts on death row."

CBS-TV football analyst John Madden on how to stop San Francisco 49ers' QB Joe Montana: "You cheat. You play 12, 13 guys. You bring in paratroopers and drop 'em from a blimp or something."

Jack Chevalier, Wilmington (Del.) News Journal sports editor, speculating that the Eagles might draft Navy running back Napoleon (Nap) McCallum: "They usually take a nap on draft day."

Merle Kessler, making a comparison: "Football players, like prostitutes, are in the business of ruining their bodies for the pleasure of strangers."

Chapter 25

Charlie Eckman, well-known Baltimore, Md. Sports personality and radio sports show host, commenting on his election bid for the 2nd District seat on the seven member Anne Arundel County Council: "I went to one debate with 24 candidates and 15 people in the stands. If it had been a football game we could've taken 'em."

Dick Enberg, NBC play-by-play announcer to analyst Bill Walsh about Herschel Walker: "He's got Clark Kent credentials, but can't get into the phone booth."

Headline on column of Baltimore (Md.) *Evening Sun* sports columnist Phil Jackman: "On New Yawn (Year) Day, Good Games Were More Slim than Lasorda's Ads."

Dan Dierdorf, ABC-TV analyst, impressed by Jimmy Johnson's going in motion and doing a 360 degree turn during the Redskin-Colts game: "My God, you need a tutu to make that kind of move."

Mike Lupica, on Notre Dame putting dollars ahead of CFA unity: "They're putting something into their fight song about how Notre Dame accepts all major credit cards."

Larry Guest, after his editor prohibited him from using nicknames like Tommy, Charlie and Bobby: "Doak Walker, the star S.M.U. half-back, has been sidelined by a Charles horse."

Paul Zimmerman, after hearing Joe Bugel blame his Phoenix Cardinals' pre-season losses on growing pains with young kids: "Does he really expect his pains to stop growing when his young kids become old kids."

*

CBS Pro football analyst Randy Cross, about big high schoolers: "Today, when you see a high school kid who's 6-7 and 275 lbs., you're not looking at a big, clumsy goof, you're looking at a potential millionaire."

*

Randy Cross, CBS—TV commentator and former 49er: "The NFL, like life, is full of idiots."

*

Sports writer, lamenting the lack of concern over education: "Some of these 19-year-olds can't read anything but a defense."

*

Dan Lebatard of the *Miami Herald* interviewing University of Miami's running back Edgerrin James after the Hurricanes spoiled UCLA's perfect season with a 49-45 win:

Q: "Describe the look on the faces of the UCLA defenders."
A: "Shocked."
Q: "Can you elaborate?"
A: "Real shocked."

*

Section IV:
The Others

Chapter 26

Joe Robbie, Miami Dolphins' G.M., on the difficulties of making a trade: "I'd cheerfully trade out No. 1 pick for a proven running back. The problem is people want an arm and a leg, and Coach Don Shula isn't willing to have an amputation."

Lulu Todd, on her first impression of Jets' QB Richard Todd, then a fellow student at Alabama and now her husband: "He dressed like a hobo, acted like God's gift to Earth and had hair longer than mine. He was real cocky and had no reason to be. He looked like Surfer Boy come to New York. A real freak-O."

Secretary of State Dean Acheson: "When the President fumbles, the whole goal line is wide open."

Reverend Jesse Jackson, on the athletic arena: "My leadership skills came from the athletic arena. In many ways, they were developed from playing quarterback. Assessing defenses; motivating your own team. When the game starts, you use what you've got—and don't cry about what you don't have. You run to your strength. You also practice to win. You really practice to win. And you tend to win if you do practice.

You learn how to lose and bounce back (in sports), and one of the qualities of leadership is resiliency. You can't take last week's tears into this week's game—and that's life, too. You must be tough enough to fight, tender enough to cry, human enough to make mistakes, humble enough to admit them, resilient enough to fight back.

These things come out of the athletic arena."

Eagles' owner Jeffrey Lurie about the option of renovating Veterans Stadium or building a new arena: "It's not good to invest in a dump unless you're in the garbage business."

🏈

Larry Bielat: "When God measures an athlete, he puts a tape around his heart, not his waist."

🏈

Headline in the *Baltimore Sun* following a Navy loss: "Fleet of mistakes sinks Navy vs. Rutgers, 28-21."

🏈

Former All-American football player, Supreme Court Justice Byron "Whizzer" White, on producing excellence: "Native ability plus formal education may be an inadequate formula to produce excellence we so urgently require. We need those mysterious and elusive qualities of courage, determination, presence of mind, self control, and concentration upon a given task."

🏈

Elbert Hatchett, lawyer for Detroit running back Billy Sims, who had signed contracts with both the Lions and the USFL's Houston Gamblers: "It makes no difference to me where Billy Sims plays football. He can play in Greenland if he can make more money there."

🏈

President Gerald Ford at the American Football Coaches Association Dinner in Washington D.C.: "I also appreciate this opportunity to be here because, as a former assistant football coach—I not only know your problems and concerns, but I've lived them. I'll never forget the time back at Yale when I went to a movie theatre with our great head coach, Ducky Pond—and the movie just happened to be that film classic *King Kong.*

Well, who can ever forget that final scene? King Kong is standing on top of the Empire State Building and men are shouting at him; women are screaming at him; the police are shooting at him; even airplanes are firing machine guns at him.

I was so impressed, I leaned over to Ducky Pond and whispered, 'When was the last time you ever saw anything like that?' Ducky said, 'Tuesday, I had a meeting with the alumni association."

❧

Theodore Roosevelt: "In life, as in a football game, the principle to follow is: Hit the line hard; don't foul and don't shrink, but hit the line hard."

❧

Novelist Tom Clancy, at a news conference regarding his possible purchase of the Minnesota Vikings, said the top item on his agenda was to deliver his next book to the publisher by April 1. Asked about the name of the book and what it was about, he replied: "It's *Rainbow Six* and it's about $24.95."

❧

Dan Marino, Sr., father of the Miami Dolphins' quarterback, Dan, Jr., on pressure: "Losing isn't life or death. The pressure of games is nothing in the scheme of things. Pressure is having six kids, and half of them sick, and you've been laid off at the mill. That's pressure."

❧

Dr. Thaddeus Seymour, former President of Wabash College, on athletics: "The generation gap cannot be closed in the classroom. It is outside, particularly in athletics, where the hard questions are asked, where a student gains the experience that will test his capacity to function as a citizen. The tremendous demands of sports on endurance and the capacity of a competitor to dig into his personal resources in a degree of willingness to sacrifice and give of the things that make for self-discipline ... it is on this quality that our society must depend if it is to survive."

❧

Robert Irsay, former owner of the Baltimore Colts: "The fella that can overcome setbacks, that can live them and knows how to go on tomorrow, he'll make it."

❧

Jean Tullai, football fan extraordinaire, upon hearing announcers constantly excusing mistakes of pro football players because they've just come into the league and are "inexperienced": "You would think they dragged these players out of the unemployment office."

❧

Scott Frederick, fine prep football official (Md.), relating a story of coaches and officials: "The angels in Heaven and the devils from below were involved in a heated discussion. Said one angel: 'Why, if we ever played a football game, we'd clobber you. After all, everybody knows that all the great coaches are here.' A devil responded, 'So what. We have all the officials down here.'"

President Gerald Ford, on football and government: "If you stop to think about it, there are many similarities between football and government. For instance, in both areas nothing is ever done without discussing it first. In football, it's called a huddle. In Washington, it's called a debate. And sometimes the talk goes on for many, many hours without really saying anything. In Washington, it's called a filibuster. In football, it's called Howard Cosell."

Johnny Walker, disc jockey, *WFBR* Baltimore: "The University of Maryland football team all make straight A's. Their B's are a little crooked."

Archibald MacLeish (Pulitzer Poetry Prize winner): "I think I learned more on the two Yale football teams I played on than I have before or since about certain very fundamental and important matters. Without more attention to things of the mind and spirit, there can be no human understanding; and that, without such understanding, the technological information which man has gathered is meaningless."

Lyndon Johnson about Gerald Ford: "Jerry Ford is a nice guy, but he played too much football without a helmet. He can't walk and chew gum at the same time."

Gerald Ford, at the Yale Law School Convocation: "It is a great pleasure—and a great honor—to be at the Yale Law School's Sesquicentennial Convocation. And I defy *anyone* to say that and chew gum at the same time!"

Dwight Eisenhower, offering a definition:
"An atheist is a guy who watches a Notre Dame-S.M.U. football game and doesn't care who wins."

🏈

Ronald Reagan, commenting on the movie in which he played George Gipp: "I saw *Knute Rockne* one night, and it was so hacked up, my eighty yard run was a five yard loss."

🏈

President Gerald Ford, at a testimonial for Congressman Sam Devine: "Sam Devine had a rather unique career. He was an F.B.I. agent, a prosecutor—and also a football referee—which can be a devastating combination. When he called a penalty, you could either lose five yards or five years."

🏈

Sally Quinn, on the football season: "The football season is like pain. You forget how terrible it is until it seizes you again."

🏈

General Douglas MacArthur, on football: "The game has become the symbol of our country's best qualities ... courage, stamina, coordinated efficiency. Many believe in these days of doubt and indecision that through this sport we can best keep alive the spirit of reality and enterprise which has made us great. Upon the fields of friendly strife are sown the seeds that, upon other fields, on other days, will bear the fruits of victory."

🏈

William Shakespeare in his *King Lear:* "You base football player."

🏈

Andrew W. White, President of Cornell University, in 1873, on football: "I will not permit 30 men to travel 400 miles merely to agitate a bag of wind."

🏈

Footballophiles about their favorite sport: "Some people think football is a matter of life and death. I don't like that attitude. I can assure you it's more serious than that."

🏈

Hubert Humphrey, trying to disassociate himself from President Johnson's Vietnam policy during the 1968 Presidential campaign: "I have not been calling the signals. I have been in the position of a lineman doing some of the downfield blocking."

Gordie Howe on pro athletes: "All pro athletes are bilingual. They speak English and profanity."

Henry L. Mencken, offering an evaluation: "It really takes no more intelligence to play football than it does to chase a cat down an alley."

Chapter 27

Long-time Atlantic Coast Conference football official upon seeing a tombstone with the inscription, "Here lies a football coach and fine man.": "How did they get two guys in the same grave?"

❦

Eugene McCarthy, former U.S. Senator: "Politics is like coaching football. You have to be smart enough to understand the game and dumb enough to think it's important."

❦

President Theodore Roosevelt on football: "I would not have football abolished for anything."

❦

T. S. Eliot, recognizing the complexities of football: "Football has become so complicated that the student will find it a recreation to go to classes."

❦

Giles Tippette in the forward of *Saturday's Children:* "Football is like your car's engine. You'll never really understand it until you've seen deep inside it and seen all its working parts at their business."

❦

Theodore Roosevelt, on athletics and academics: "It is not healthy for either students or athletes if the terms are mutually exclusive."

❦

Jack Lavelle, the great scout for the New York Giants, after scouting the Baltimore Colts: "I'm glad we don't have to play the Colt fans. They're tougher than the team."

❦

Bert Bell, when asked during his stint as pro football commissioner, what would happen if, when the extra point kick was being attempted, the ball burst in the air with half going over the bar and half under: "Well, the way I see it, the team would be out at least 18 bucks."

❧

Ernie Accorsi, on advice received from Joe Paterno while Accorsi was at Penn State: "I'll never forget Joe looking at me and saying, 'It doesn't matter where you are when you're 18 or 35. It's where you've been when you're 65.'"

❧

Ronald Reagan, on his football playing experience: "I never thought seriously about retiring from the junior mayhem, but I managed to time my charge so that I was in one of the upper layers of bodies. The lure of sweat and action always pulled me back to the game—despite the fact that I was a scrawny, undersized, underweight nuisance, who insisted on getting in the way of the more skillful (such as my brother). As a result, I had a collection of the largest purplish-black bruises possible. More than once, I must have been a walking coagulation. Those were the happiest times of my life."

❧

Norman Hackerman, President of Rice, after the Owls signed new football coach Watson Brown to a six-year contract reportedly worth $1.2 million: "It's a commentary on society, not me."

❧

Comedian Bob Hope on his football experience: "I was known as Neckline Hope. I was always plunging down the middle, but never really showing anything."

❧

Actor Gary Busey, on what Dallas Cowboys' coach Tom Landry told him about how to play the late Paul "Bear" Bryant in a movie based on the Bear's life: "He said it's all in how you wear the hat."

❧

Ron Stanko, attorney for Baltimore Colts' Derrick Hatchett, regarding Hatchett's contract obligations with the Colts: "Indentured servants went out with the Gettysburg Address."

Pete Rozelle, NFL Commissioner, on whether the Chicago Bears would be asked to move from antiquated Soldier Field: "We have to defer to George Halas or else he might take his league back."

Oliver Pierce, assistant sports information director, after Washington State was awarded forfeit football victories in 1977, '78, and '79: "We're now waiting for a retroactive Rose Bowl bid."

President Gerald R. Ford, who played center and linebacker at the University of Michigan and is the only President ever to play in a national All-Star football game (Aug. 29, 1935): "I only wish that I could take the entire United States into the locker room at half time. I would simply say that we must look not at the points we have lost, but at the points we can gain."

Lubbock Christian College Athletic Director after firing the football coach: "He's a great guy, but we can take only so many great lessons in humility."

Mark McCormack, sports superagent, defining his role: "I'm not an agent. I'm an engineer of careers."

H. Ross Perot, Dallas electronics magnate and head of the Texas select Committee on Public Education: "Are we in school or are we in show business? I don't think football has anything to do with education. If Rice were to drop football altogether, the sun would still rise in the morning."

Redskin owner, Jack Kent Cooke, whose fortune is estimated to be in excess of $600 million, on his team: "It was a thrill to light the Chrysler Building [which he bought for $92 million] and it's gratifying to own half of downtown Phoenix. There's all of that, but his is fun! There's nothing remotely matching the stupendous, smashing, stunning hobby of the Redskins."

Laurence Stallings, who wrote *What Price Glory* and *The Big Parade,* after witnessing Red Grange's spectacular performance against Pennsylvania—three touchdowns, 363 yards in 36 carries—tore up the copy he had typed, walked out of the press box and declared: "It's too big; I can't write it. I've never seen a sight like that."

NFL scout, upon learning that John Washington had changed his name to John Jefferson upon enrolling at Arizona State: "Why did he skip John Adams?"

Art Modell, owner of the Cleveland Browns, on the USFL: "I give them high marks for the courage of their convictions. But they are committing hara-kiri and murder at the same time."

One referee's answer on why a coach would be received in Heaven more enthusiastically than a Bishop: "They probably get a Bishop a week there. But the next coach will be the first."

Author Elbert Hubbard, characterizing football: "Football—a sport that bears the same relationship to education that bullfighting does to agriculture."

Theodore Roosevelt on making an effort: "It is not the critic who counts; not the man who points out how the strong man stumbles, or where the door of deeds could have done them better. The credit belongs to the man who is actually in the arena, whose face is marred by dust and sweat and blood; who strives valiantly; who errs, and comes short again and again, because there is no effort without error and shortcoming; but who does actually strive to do the deeds; who knows the great enthusiasms, the great devotions; who spends himself in a worthy cause; who at the best knows in the end the triumph of high achievement, and who at the worst, if he fails, at least fails while daring greatly, so that his place shall never be with those cold and timid souls who know neither victory nor defeat."

President Dwight D. Eisenhower, on football: "I believe that football instills into many men the feeling that victory comes through hard—almost slavish—work, team play, self-confidence, and an enthusiasm that amounts to dedication."

🏈

Sir Walter Scott, Scottish poet and novelist (1771-1832), in "Song": "Then, strip, lads, and to it, though sharp be the weather,
And if, by mischance, you should happen to fall,
There are worst things in life that a tumble on heather,
And life is itself but a game at football."

🏈

Paul Light, Director of Studies for the National Academy of Public Administration, on the Vice President: "A Vice President can't take credit for administration successes. It's like the water boy on a football team claiming that he was responsible for the victory when everybody saw the quarterback on television running the show."

🏈

Anonymous British fan, viewing the Minnesota Vikings 28-10 victory over St. Louis in the first NFL game every played in London: "It takes them an hour to play 20 minutes. And why is the referee always dropping yellow dusters on the field?"

🏈

Haywood Hale Brown, on character: "Sports do not build character, they reveal it."

🏈

Art Modell, Baltimore Ravens' owner, on the prospects of back-up QB Stoney Case: "Stoney turned into a pebble. I don't think he's the answer."

🏈

Jean Tullai, an astute football observer from Lutherville, Md., upon reading that Stoney Case would open the 2000 season as the Detroit Lions' starting QB: "Well, I guess Stoney just became a boulder."

🏈

Governor-elect Roy Barnes of Georgia, on his future, after doing the sports on an Atlanta television station's nightly news: "I don't believe I'll quit my day job."

Chapter 28

Gerald R. Ford, about his 1934 Michigan football team that lost seven of its first eight games—five by shutouts: "Frankly as individuals, we were God-fearing—but as a team, we didn't have a prayer."

New Orleans Saint fan Arlene Hall, after seeing a last-second L. A. Ram field goal knock her team out of an NFL play-off berth: "We all must have done something horrible in a previous life. God doesn't want us to win."

Charlton Heston, movie actor, on learning the art of quarterbacking: "It took me three months to learn to ride a chariot for 'Ben Hur.' I learned about painting in a few weeks to play Michelangelo in 'The Agony and the Ecstasy.' And being Moses in the 'Ten Commandments' and parting the Red Sea with the help of Cecil B. DeMille and God took no time at all. But it took me more than eight months to remotely resemble pro quarterback, the hardest preparation I ever had for a film ['Number One']. Learning to step up in a pocket in the face of a pass rush is against every human instinct. Every nerve in your body is saying, 'Keep going, get rid of the ball.'"

James Michener, author, on the historical figure he pitied most: "General Custer—imagine having to watch the game film next day!"

President John F. Kennedy, on football: "I sometimes wonder whether those of us who love football fully appreciate its great lessons: That dedication, discipline, and teamwork are necessary to success. We take it for granted that the players will spare no sacrifice to become alert, strong, and skilled—that they will give their best on the field. This is as it should be, and we must never expect less, but I am extremely anxious that its implications not be lost on us."

President Gerald Ford, on introductions: "Let me thank Chris Schenkel for that fine introduction. You know, since I became President, I'm usually introduced in a very stately and dignified manner—such as tonight. But there was one dinner when I was introduced by a former teammate of mine from my old Michigan football team—and I'll never forget that introduction. He said, 'Ladies and Gentlemen, it might interest you to know that I played football with Jerry Ford for two years—and it made a lasting impression on me. I was quarterback. Jerry Ford was the center. And you might say, it gave me a completely different view of the President!'"

Thoughts from the 16th century on football: "... nothing but beastly furie and exstreme violence; whereof procedeth hurte, and consequently rancour and malice do remaine with that he wounded."

Johnny Carson, during his Thanksgiving Day monologue, after the Detroit Lions beat the Pittsburgh Steelers, 45 to 3: "I'll tell you what my Thanksgiving has been like—I had the Steelers and only 40 points."

President Ronald Reagan, to Tom Flores, coach of the L. A. Raiders' Super Bowl champions: "Congratulations, that was a wonderful win. I think you ought to know I just received a call from Moscow. They think Marcus Allen is a new secret weapon and they insist we dismantle him."
—and—
You've given me an idea with that team of yours. If you'd turn them over to us, we'd put them in silos and we wouldn't have to build the MX missile."

Admiral Jonas Ingram, on football: "Looking back over the years, the results of football training are most convincing. I know of no athletic competition that develops more useful traits of character or essential physical prowess. For example: the subordination of the individual to team play, development of initiative, leadership, and the value of persistence and physical fitness, the self-determination that inspires 'the will to win' against any odds—and along with it all, the building of real character and true sportsmanship."

Robert Finch, California's former lieutenant governor, urging residents to offer housing to visiting midshipmen and cadets when the Army-Navy game is played in Pasadena: "These fine young men and women are the best kind of guests. They're experts at making their own beds."

Randy Cross, game analyst, during the Baltimore-Pittsburgh contest, which had much pushing and shoving after the whistle: "They'd be better off doing that between whistles rather than after the whistle."

President Gerald R. Ford, on being ready: "We must be physically and mentally fit because the times demand that we not only compete but that we excel, and we must do it with enthusiasm, the enthusiasm found more prominently on the field of sport."

Marcus Cunliffe, British historian and observer of American affairs, on football and politics: "It is tempting to speculate that the national game of politics has influenced the development of the American version of football, which is elaborate, ritualized, episodic, somewhat arcane and therefore difficult for a novice to follow, and has a sort of jackpot quality in which a sudden profusion of points may be scored. Possession of the ball is highly important; fumbling may be disastrous and give possession to the other team (party). The side that has possession must give proof of the ability to gain ground or it will automatically lose possession to the other side. The most important performer in these games is a non-player, the coach, whose direction is, according to temperament, sometimes flamboyantly apparent and sometimes cooly concealed. The contract of an unsuccessful coach is not renewed. One might add other analogies: for example that, other things being equal, the richest team is the likeliest to rise to the head of the table."

Burt Reynolds, on Howard Cosell: "In the next issue of *Cosmopolitan*, Howard Cosell will be the centerfold with his vital organ covered—his mouth."

Al LoCasale, Al Davis' right-hand man with the L. A. Raiders on failing TV ratings: "Ratings always fluctuate. Look at the U. S. Government. They were in Grenada and the ratings shot up. If we could find some island with 200 people with blowguns to invade, our ratings would go up, too."

Art Modell, owner of the Cleveland Browns, on NFL franchise shifts: "A sports franchise has a responsibility to a community that transcends putting on a good team. It's part of the landscape, more important than a museum or the orchestra."

Governor Lee S. Dreyfus of Wisconsin (a former college president) on athletics: "There's no program in any school system that does for the issue of racial equality what athletics does. It teaches you to judge a human being on his competence and his performance."

An old grad's response after Indiana's student-body president suggested that all prisoners of war should be admitted free to Hoosier football games: "I am opposed to this. These fellows have suffered enough."

Dick Rudolph, former City College (MD) football player and successful businessman: "A loser is a person who has too much wishbone and too little backbone."

Comedian Henny Youngman, on his experience as a football spectator: "I went out to see a football game, but from where I sat the game was only a rumor. I was up so high I kept getting spirit messages. When the usher got me halfway up, he said, 'You'll have to go the rest of the way yourself. From here on my nose bleeds.' Finally I said to a guy next to me, 'How do you like the game?' He says, 'What game? I'm flying the mail to Pittsburgh.'"

News item on the marketing of a new drink: "A new drink being marketed to commemorate the Notre Dame-Miami game Sept. 24 in the Orange Bowl is called the Irish Hurricane. If consists of Irish Crème liqueur, rum and orange juice and is said to be powerful enough to fuel the Concorde."

Jack Elway, on marrying the perfect kind of woman to produce an athlete like John Elway: "My friends tell me that I was an over-achiever when I got married."

Ed Croke, New York Giants' public relations man on 295-lb. defensive end, Leonard Marshall: "We put him on a Cambridge diet, and he ate half of Cambridge."

Morris Udall, Arizona Congressman, on Walter Mondale's selection of Geraldine Ferraro as his Vice Presidential running mate: "He went for the big play—and it might work."

Will Rogers, humorist, answering the question, does college pay?: "They do if you are a good open-field runner."

Howard Slusher, agent for Mike Haynes, about the New England Patriots giving away 15,000 tickets in their season opener: "They're like a World Football League team. Only World Football League teams give away tickets."

General George C. Marshall, Chief of Staff during World War II, instructing an aide: "I want an officer for a secret and dangerous mission. I want a West Point football player."

Richard Nixon, on football: "I never made the football team ... I was not heavy enough to play the line, not fast enough to play halfback, and not smart enough to be quarterback."

Erma Bombeck, syndicated columnist, on "bowling": "The Rose Bowl is the only bowl I've ever seen that I didn't have to clean."

Chapter 29

President Woodrow Wilson, on football: "I have always thought it was an accepted fact that football was an educational factor ... To excel personally and collectively to win, a player must mobilize into action judgment, persistence, initiative, aggressiveness, fortitude, courage, chivalry and the will to win. Repeatedly doing so makes these acts traits of his own character. Spectators seeing these traits copy them. These are basic traits of character essential to success in any endeavor. Therefore, to my mind, football is pre-eminently an educational factor."

Washington Redskins owner Edward Bennett Williams, on Coach George Allen's budget: "I have given him an unlimited budget, and he's already exceeded it."

Author Dan Jenkins about football: "God invented football so grown men would have something to do between wars."

Oakland Raider fan: "The season ain't over until the fat boys sit down."

President John Kennedy, on winning: "Victory has a hundred fathers, defeat is an orphan."

Dr. Norman Vincent Peale, on sports: "Jesus always followed what most interested the people. He talked about the lessons found in everyday life. You can be sure He would find many lessons in American sports. He taught all of the qualities that make for good sports: discipline, courage, health, cleanliness, mental awareness, and the rest."

Admiral Thomas Hamilton, on football: "Football is a game where not only the whole team must act right, but think right, and believe right—together as a team. The violation of a rule brings a costly penalty, and courage is required not only for the physical, but also to control one's temper and individual impulses. It has an emotionalism and a surge which stirs players and spectators alike. The drama and closeness of the cause pull a squad or school together, and teammates are brothers indeed. Pride in accomplishment is a key factor for team success, and the fear of failing one's teammates produces skills and performances the player never knew he possessed."

Oklahoma Sports Information Director, John Keith, on the Heisman Trophy:

"1. He has to play at a 'recognized football school'—and there are only about 15 of them in the land.

2. He has to have a great year.

3. He has to pray that Notre Dame doesn't have someone."

Robert Irsay, Baltimore Colts' owner commenting on offense guard Ken Huff's contract hold-out: "We told him to go out and find himself a trade. We were willing. He hasn't. We made him a generous offer and he threw it back in my face. The monkey is on his shoe now."

Johnny Carson, on Vince Ferragamo's bitter contract negotiations with Georgia Rosenbloom of the Rams: "Georgia won't give him a raise, but she's willing to marry him."

Bob Hope, on the power running of the L. A. Raiders' Marcus Allen: "He carries so many tacklers with him, he's noted in the yellow pages under 'Public Transportation.'"

Bernie Ulman, a top college lacrosse and football official and NFL referee, when asked how he felt being booed by fans at a Navy-Johns Hopkins lacrosse game: "Heck, there are only 5,000 people here. I've been booed before by 80,000 experts [in the Los Angeles Coliseum].

Cincinnati Bengal fan, reflecting the view that the team's decline paralleled the rise of the intellectual football player: "The Bengals need some players who speak only one-syllable words, eat bananas, and have to be chained to the bench."

Mrs. Janet Elway, on her famous son, John: "Everybody thinks John was born with a silver spoon in his mouth, but it was more like a stainless steel one, and believe me, he's never been on a surfboard."

Bob Newhardt, describing his brief high school career as a halfback: "When I went into the line on a fake, I'd holler, 'I don't have it, I don't have it.'"

Legend on a poster featuring Navy's ace running back and Heisman Trophy candidate, Napoleon McCallum, dressed in an 18th century naval uniform: "I have not yet begun to run."

Jean Bell, a keen observer of the gridiron scene from Lutherville, Md., on criticism: "Don't blame the coach for being a crank if you're not a self-starter."

John Kulas, on how Boston College managed to recruit the most exciting little man in NCAA football, 5'9" Doug Flutie, who had not been recruited by any other Division I college: "As a Jesuit school, B. C. gets its scouting reports from a higher authority."

John Chamberlain, editor, essayist, and critic, on football: "Far from being overemphasized, football may be the school's most enduring contact with the world of discipline, of sharp thinking, of a demonstrable connection between what one puts into a thing and what one gets out of it at the other end. Let's have more of it."

George Young, New York Giants' General Manager, on player negotiations: "It is all negotiating palaver. Players send in their agents who surround you with illogic. They give you reasons why with words that are designed to get money out of you."

A Forty-Niners executive's comment after Fred Dean's contract demands of deferred payments over 25 years, life and health insurance for the next 25 years, two round-trip airline tickets from either Shreveport, La. or San Diego to all 49-er games, two suites at all away games in which he competes and a room and meal money the entire week before any future Super Bowls in which the 49-ers compete: "That's not a contract. Those are adoption papers. He is filing to be known as Freddie DeBartolo."

Bob Hope, on hearing that the U. S. Post Office would be represented in the Rose Bowl Parade on January 1st: "You can bet that their float will reach the judges' stand by January 6th."

Gene Klein, San Diego Chargers' owner, on one of the reasons he would like to sell his football team and turn his interest to horses rather than continue to deal with the contract hassles in football: "At least the horses don't talk back."

Jets' team doctor, on what a player should do if he ever breaks his leg in two places: "Never go back to those places."

Bob Springer, old time West Virginia footballer and knowledgeable fan, on the value of the wave cheer: "It gets boring after a while, but it does straighten out your shorts."

Gerald Ford, on his football days: "I had pro offers from the Detroit Lions and Green Bay Packers, who were pretty hard up for linemen in those days. If I had gone into professional football, the name Jerry Ford might have been a household word today."

George Young, N. Y. Giants' General Manager, on the NFL's physical testing day for college draftees: "It's a day for the guys who look good in their underwear."

🏈

Tom Brokaw, NBC-TV anchorman, addressing the NCAA's honors luncheon as its master of ceremonies: "I'm honored that you invited me, especially when for $10,000 and a new convertible you could have had the top running back prospect at S.M.U."

🏈

Buddy Baron, Cincinnati disc jockey, on the Chicago Bears use of acupuncture: "Good thing William Perry didn't need it. They'd have to use a harpoon."

🏈

David Letterman, commenting on the USFL antitrust lawsuit against NFL in Federal District Court in New York: "There were 150 people in the courtroom—third largest crowd ever to see the USFL in action."

🏈

Larry Munro, agent for Tory Nixon drafted by Washington, after Redskins' owner Jack Kent Cooke gave Nixon an ultimatum to sign a final reduced offer: "Cooke believes in the golden rule: 'He who has the gold, rules.'"

🏈

Jacques Barzum, on watching a game: "To watch a football game is to be in prolonged neurotic doubt as to what you're seeing. It is more like an emergency happening at a distance than a game. I don't wonder the spectators take to drink."

🏈

Frank Broyles, Arkansas Athletic Director, on whether he'd still like his football coach, Ken Hatfield, if the team won only half its games: "Sure I would. I'd miss him, too."

🏈

Lamar Hunt after being burned a number of times by the legal profession: "My idea of an utter waste is a busload of lawyers going over a cliff with three empty seats."

Bill Callahan, University of Missouri sports information director, on how he improved at his job: "I used to have the worst time remembering names. Then I took the Sam Carnegie Course and I've been all right ever since."

Louis D. Clark, historian, Thomas Jefferson scholar and knowledgeable football observer: "Offensive football is enjoyable. But the defensive players stand out because they appreciate life, liberty and the happiness of pursuit."

Chapter 30

Bob Cooper, respected football arbiter (Baltimore, Md.), about being a referee: "That's one thing about officiating. I never get lost. Everyone tells me where to go."

Harry Truman, making a comparison: "It's a lot tougher to be a football coach than a President. You've got four years as a President, and they guard you. A coach doesn't have anyone to protect him when things go wrong."

George F. Will, syndicated columnist, noting the number of officiating conferences on the field every Sunday: "Football continues to combine the two worst features of American life—violence and committee meetings."

Utah sports information director Bruce Woodbury's comment, after writers in the press box suggested that a naked woman who ran onto the field before the Texas-El Paso-Utah game and reclined on the 50-yard line until police took her away, ought to be taken to a mental hospital: "I think she has already been under enough observation."

Fans cheer at Duke University after losing a football game: "Hey, hey, that's O.K. You're going to work for us someday."

President George Bush, in Notre Dame's swift, running back, Raghib "Rocket" Ismail: "The best use of speed since Chuck Yeager broke the sound barrier."

Press joke at Texas Stadium: "Will the woman who has lost her 11 kids here at Texas Stadium, please report to the field—they're beating the Cowboys, 14-0."

Ernie Accorsi, New York Giants General Manager, about his high school team: "What a team! We once played a game where our opponents walked off the field because they objected to the officiating. Three plays later we scored—on a partially blocked field goal."

Comedian Phil Foster advising Frank Gifford on how to beat Art Donovan: "As soon as you get the ball, throw Donovan a six pack."

The *San Diego Union,* in a profile of Jack Kent Cooke, relating an "old boardroom joke" offered by one NFL owner to describe the Washington owner: "He fell off a yacht into a school of sharks, but they didn't touch him. Professional courtesy."

Roger Simon, *Baltimore Sun* columnist: "I don't miss pro football. I have always liked college football better. It's more exciting, and the players make slightly less."

Johnny Carson, late night show host: "The last time the Browns were in a play-off, Cleveland wasn't a city, it was a President."

Linus Pauling, a chemist and two-time Nobel Prize winner, asked what he does to relax: "I take a glass of vodka, turn on the TV, and watch a football game."

Johnny Carson to Howard Cosell: "If I were Paul Revere, I'd never warn you."

White House spokesman Larry Speakes commenting on the Reykjavik summit where a potential agreement on an arms treaty fell apart over "Star Wars" testing following a five hour overtime session between Reagan and Gorbachev: "The two sides went 99 yards ... but we didn't cross the goal line."

🏈

Steve Sabol, head of NFL Films describing the most impressive player he ever saw on film: "Dick Butkus—he was like Moby Dick in a goldfish bowl."

🏈

Cincinnati Mayor Charles chc, who lost a bet to Cleveland Mayor George Voinovich that the Bengals would beat the Browns in their December 14 meeting, on why he waited a week to pay off—to fly the Cleveland flag about Cincinnati's City Hall for one day: "I looked it up and December 21 is the shortest day of the year."

🏈

Mrs. Tom Landry, on why the Landry marriage is in such good shape: "I'm near-sighted and Tom is far-sighted. So I read the menus and he reads the street signs."

🏈

Art Modell, Cleveland Browns' owner, about the three hour, 53 minute marathon game between the Redksins and 49ers: "If my wife (a former actress) had a series that ran that long, she'd still be on television."

🏈

Cleveland left tackle Ricky Bolden's fiancee, after he was called for five holding penalties: "You don't even hold me that much."

🏈

Bumper sticker in Georgia: "Go Braves ... and take the Falcons with you."

🏈

Tex Schramm, president of the World League of American Football, on one problem he doesn't figure to have the first year: "I won't be worried about crowd noise."

NFL Films president Steve Sabol, characterizing the differences between fans of opposing Super Bowl XXX teams Dallas and Pittsburgh: "Neiman Marcus versus True Value Hardware."

Braggart in stands at a football game: "When I was in college, I helped Harvard beat Yale three times in succession."
John Barrymore: "That so? Which team were you playing on?"

Football player's wife: "I hate it when my husband calls leftovers 'replays.'"

Art Modell, Cleveland Browns' owner, jokingly, after a slow start prompted fans to put up critical signs including, "Larry, Curly and Modell": "The only thing that bothered me about that is one night I got up and saw my wife painting the signs."

Rodney Dangerfield, on his sports experience: "My father wanted me to be a ball player, but the first time he played ball with me he dropped me."

George Young, General Manager of the New York Giants, when he heard agent Leigh Steinberg had thrown a party for the media during Super Bowl week: "When I heard he was taking all those writers out on a river boat, I spent about an hour trying to rent a submarine."

Willie Monetti, on reading that Staurovsky and Stoyonovich kicked field goals for Nebraska and Miami respectively: "Was it the NCAA or World Cup '90?"

Al Hunt, Washington correspondent of the Wall Street Journal on why domestic problems were not being given a lot of attention by the Bush Administration: "The Persian Gulf has really frozen the line-backers."

🏈

Ralph Campbell, one of the Hogettes, the unofficial male Redskin cheerleaders, who dress up as women, on his group's wardrobe: "Our designer is Calvin Swine."

🏈

Some names the Detroit fans selected for the Lions run-and-shoot offense after the team got off to a losing start: "The Run and Hide"; "The Shoot and Miss"; "The Third and So Long"

🏈

Mark Preston, TV critic, evaluating Jim Lampley: "He is so stiff out there on HBO that people are gonna begin hanging coats on him."

🏈

Representative John Reid, discussing his Holiday Bowl Committee blazer (flaming red): "I try not to wear it in hotel lobbies. People keep trying to give me their luggage."

🏈

Jim Greenridge, the Patriots 320 lb. P. R. man, on when he realized he had a weight problem: "When the team sent me to a Kentucky Fried Chicken place for two double large baskets and the attendant asked, 'To stay or to go.'"

🏈

Bob Hope about the Chicago Bears: "The Bears are so intimidating that when the opponents win the toss they always elect to go home."

🏈

Nick DeSoto, discerning 12th Grade student in a Presidential course at St. Paul's School (Brooklandville, MD) on why he should make George H. W. Bush (father) the Quarterback on his "Presidential All American Football Team": "When he calls a check-off and there is a lot of crowd noise, the whole team will be able to 'read his lips.'"

🏈

Section V:
Special Personality
Art Donovan

"Artie Donovan has become a folk hero by doing what comes natural, telling stories"

-John Eisenberg, Sports Columnist
Baltimore Sun

"Artie Donovan is absolutely the funniest banquet speaker I have ever heard"

-Vince Bagli, former Sports Director
WBAL TV, Baltimore MD

Art Donovan: Story-Teller and Wit Extraordinaire

The National Football League has seen some great football players and some great funny men. However, the best combination of great player and great wit is exemplified by Arthur Donovan. A Baltimore Colt legend and Hall of Famer, he is one of the funniest men around. Columnist Sylvia Badger of the *Baltimore News American* has written about this amiable giant: "You don't have to be a football nut to enjoy Donovan's antics"—"he's a natural comedian."

Many of the following repartees are with noted sportscaster Phil Wood, host of *WCBM's* (Baltimore) "Monday Night Football," and with guests who visited the show.

On exhibition games: "Exhibitions are for coaches and for losers:

Discussing a Colt player with Phil Wood:
Donovan: "That one Colt tackle is pretty good. I can't pronounce his name—it's so long it runs off his jersey."
Wood: "Baldischwiler."
Donovan: "Who?"
Wood: "Baldischwiler."
Donovan: "Yeah, yeah. He's an Irishman."

On offensive linemen: "Slow feet, quick hands! Where do they get all that stuff? They all look like octupuses."

Donovan, after explaining the difference between a muff and a fumble: "I didn't know I knew so much about the rules. I was just a dumb tackle. I never read the rule book."
Phil Wood: "Osmosis?"
Donovan: "Osmosis? Who'd he play for?"

Groping for a coach's name: "What was the name of the Buffalo coach—oh yeah, Kay Kyser." (Actually, Kay Stephenson)

On drafting players: "If you draft first, you have to go with the quarterback from Stanford—Fauntleroy." (Actually, Elway)

On coach Ted Marchibroda's optimistic outlook about the Baltimore Colts: "If he's in his right mind, he's crazy."

Phil Wood to Colt kicker, Raul Allegre: "I notice you wear sweat pants on the sideline."
Donovan: "Yeah, they're a sexy looking pair of bloomers. You look like Ricardo Montalban."

Following several weird and crazy phone calls on *WCBM:* "It's got to be a Christmas party or there's a full moon tonight."

About his old coach Weeb Ewbank: "Ewbank is a smart guy. If they'd made Weeb a spy in World War II instead of a football coach, he'd a had Russia so screwed up we'd never have to worry about them."

About a speech by President Reagan that would pre-empt a portion of the "Monday Night Live" show on *WCBM* (Baltimore, Md.): "If I'd a known he was going to do this, I would never have watched his movies."

Describing Big Daddy Lipscomb's method of defensive line play: "He'd grab a whole armful of guys with the other color jersey. Then he'd peel them off 'til he found the one with the ball."

On officiating: "I saw an official yesterday call a face-masking penalty from 80 yards away. He couldn't have seen the play if he had binoculars."

On statistics: "Statistics are for losers and coaches."

On Mark Hermann, the Colts' 6'5" quarterback: "Hermann is no more nifty than I am. Did you ever see me dance? Did you ever see an elephant dance?"

On jogging: "No, I don't jog. When I die I want to be sick."

On John Unitas: "John Unitas was a great quarterback. There are only a few guys you can mention in his breath."

Donovan to Phil Wood: "Sometimes I think you don't understand my wit, Phil."
Phil Wood: "I'm not the only one, Arthur."

On former Colt great Bill Pellington, regarded by Donovan and others as one of the toughest, most determined players ever to play pro football: "Bill Pellington hit Bill Houghton of the Packers so hard, Houghton appealed to the officials: 'Why don't you give him a gun and let him finish the job?'"

After the 1983 Colts beat Philadelphia, 22-21 and stood at a 5-4 record: "This is a miracle—like the Lady of Fatima."

Donovan to Coach Frank Kush:
"Coach, what's wrong with your kicker, Raul Allegre?"
Kush: "He's got a right hip flexor."
Donovan: What! That sounds like a swear word—in Italian."

Asked to comment on sex and football: "Why ask *me* a question like that. With my face and my body, I'm lucky my kids even kiss me."

Relating a Ewbank-Unitas story: "John came to the sideline during a third and 12 situation and says to Weeb, 'Coach, what do you have?' Ewbank says, 'What?' Unitas says, 'What do you have—what play shall I do?' Ewbank looks at the crowd, looks around, turns to Unitas and says: "Get a first down.'"

*

To Phil Wood, his partner on *WCBM* "Monday Night Football," after the Colts lost to the Giants (10-6) and had a record of 6-8 and Wood said, "The Colts can still make the play-offs.": "Make the play-offs! They ought to have the Colts and the N. Y. Giants in a bowl—the 'Toilet Bowl!'"

*

On coaches: "These coaches—I'm not calling them liars, but a lot of them circumvent the truth."

*

Phil Wood to Donovan about Zach Dixon, a Colt running back: "He was just trying to be humble, Arthur."
Donovan: "Aw, humble my foot. Humble is the name of a gas station."

*

On obtaining information: "I don't always read the papers and believe what I hear."

*

To Frank Kush, about Mark Hermann, the Colts' tall and thin quarterback: "Mark Hermann is 6'5", 180 lbs. Boy, oh boy, Coach, you'd better get him a suit of armor."

*

Speaking about himself and former Colt defensive end, Ordell Braase: "We're just two ex has-beens."

*

Giving advice to first year tackle Jim Parker (later to become a Hall of Famer) as to what he should do about Gino Marchetti, who had beaten him on the previous three plays: "Shucks, Jim, if I were you, I'd applaud."

*

On predicting: "You want me to predict the results of Sunday games. Hey predicting is hard. Especially about the future."

*

Commenting on the fact that Don Shula lost the 1983 Super Bowl to the Redskins: "They said Shula could walk on water, but he missed a rock that day."

Regarding the pigeons in and around Baltimore's Memorial Stadium: "It's better than San Francisco where they have sea gulls. Sea gulls drop bigger bombs."

Donovan and Ordell Braase, in classic repartee, during a radio talk show: *Braase:* "Arthur, I noticed that Coach Marchibroda had his entire coaching staff with him at the Booster Club meeting."
Donovan: "Hey, when you're 1 and 4, you don't go anywhere by yourself."

Donovan and Braase, bantering about their college experiences: *Braase:* "My coach used to have bed check for me every night."
Donovan: "Yeah, what happened?"
Braase: "No problem, my bed was always there."

Donovan and Braase, about defense: *Donovan:* "Hey, O'dell, why don't you tell the folks about playing defense—it won't take long."
Braase: "I'll tell all we both know, Arthur—it won't take any longer."

About Roger Carr, who was traded by the Colts to San Diego: "Coach Mike McCormack got rid of Roger Carr. Boy watch San Diego go down. He'd ruin eleven apostles playing together."

On Jim Smith, the New England Patriot kicker who missed two field goals and two extra points against the Baltimore Colts: "He must have been thinking about Pocahontas."

Peter Jay, contributing columnist for the *Baltimore Sun*, recognizing that Arthur Donovan's answer about the Colts' departure for Indianapolis was "that of a man wiser than most," when Donovan said: "Naw, it wasn't a tragedy. When a young kid dies or gets crippled, that's tragedy. The Colt's leaving was just a happening."

Index

Index

Index

Index

Index

Index

Index

Index

Index

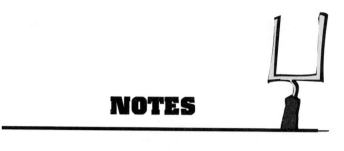

NOTES

ORDER FORM

PEARCE PUBLISHERS, INC.
P.O. Box 4923
Timonium, MD 21094
toll free: 1-800-662-2354

Ship to:	Bill to: (if different than shipping)
Name	Name
Address	Address
City St. Zip	City St. Zip
Day Phone ( )	Day Phone ( )

Quantity	Title/Author	Price Each	Total Price
	Football's Best	$16.95	
	Quips, Quotes andQuellers		
	by Martin D. (Mitch) Tullai		

Did you remember to?		
√ Print your Name, Address, Zip code & phone #	**Subtotal**	
√ Enclose payment or charge account number	**Sales Tax**	
√ Signature for charge order	**S & H**	
	Total	

Enclose your money order or personal check

Money Order   Personal Check

Shipping Schedule
All orders shipped UPS.
No. P.O. Boxes.
USA shipments only.

Cost	S & H
$16-$45	$6.50
over $45	call

Signature